The life of Musorgsky

Musical lives

The books in this series each provide an
account of the life of a major composer,
considering both the private and the public
figure. The main thread is biographical and
discussion of the music is integral to the
narrative. Each book thus presents an
organic view of the composer, the music,
and the circumstances in which the music
was written.

Published titles

CONTENTS

ILLUSTRATIONS

All illustrations with exception of nos. 11, 17 and 18 are reproduced
courtesy Muzyka Publishers, Moscow. Nos 17 and 18 are reproduced
courtesy Iskusstvo Publishers, Moscow. No. 11 is reproduced
courtesy Edizioni del Teatro Alla Scala, Milan.

Musorgsky was an excellent prose stylist and a crafty, idiosyncratic letter-writer, one of the best among Russia's great nineteenth-century creative artists. Almost all personal letters and Russian-language memoirs drawn upon in this biography can be found in the two serviceable English-language editions below. The persistent reader will discover, however, that no translation appears in my narrative precisely as it exists in the English source. Inaccuracies in these published versions have been corrected and many passages have been wholly recast for intonation and style. All translations have been verified against their original languages in authoritative Russian editions.

For the letters: *The Musorgsky Reader: a Life of Modeste Petrovich Musorgsky in Letters and Documents*, ed. and trans. Jay Leyda and Sergei Bertensson (New York: Da Capo Press, orig. 1947/repr. 1970). A chronological arrangement of the letters, with helpful biographical glosses. In text, L.

For memoir accounts: Alexandra Orlova, ed., *Musorgsky Remembered*, trans. Véronique Zaytzeff and Frederick Morrison (Bloomington: Indiana University Press, 1991). Excerpts from major reminiscences by Musorgsky's friends, mentors, contemporaries, critics, and admirers. In text, MR.

Letters and memoirs will not be individually footnoted in the text of the biography if they can be found in one of the two volumes above. Parenthetical reference after the cited letter will be made to L, followed by page number; for memoirs, to MR.

ACKNOWLEDGMENTS

To my husband, Ivan Zaknic, the usual loving gratitude for doing everything that needs to be done while I do this. Constance Cooper, composer, pianist, and for a decade my co-performer of Musorgsky's cycles and songs, has allowed me to taste what it must have been like making chamber music in the infinitely more literate – and leisurely – world of nineteenth-century Russian culture. Warm thanks to Penny Souster of Cambridge University Press, an editor both patient and wise.

My own writing about Musorgsky has greatly benefited by working with Robert William Oldani, musicologist and music historian, on our co-authored *Modest Musorgsky and Boris Godunov: Myths, Realities, Reconsiderations* (Cambridge University Press, 1994). His precision in research was exemplary for me in the present project and his notations on its final drafts indispensable. But the reconstruction of a creative life, even in short compass, is of another order of magnitude and audacity than the explication of an artistic text. Caution is necessary at every point. And never more so than in a biography that sets for its goal that most difficult mean: not to lose the general reader while not embarrassing the professional one. My final debts, therefore, are of two sorts.

First, I am grateful to my five "lay" readers – music lovers and Slavists – who went carefully over all chapters of the manuscript, providing excellent commentary, advice, and calls to discipline: Kathleen Parthé, Inessa Medzhibovskaya, Amy Mandelker, Nicole Monnier, and Olga Peters Hasty. And then there are the two music professionals in whose wake I have long been pleased to trail: Richard Taruskin, whose luminescent writings on Russian music have reconfigured the field, and my father David Geppert, retired from the Eastman School of Music, to whom I owe whatever passion for music I have been able to cultivate and who contributed the "Musical Postlude" for the present volume. To these two communicants and mentors I dedicate this book.

It is a rare biography that does not claim, at some point, the impenetrability of its subject. This is no exception. But such routine disclaimers – that we cannot see the hero, that he is hidden from the world – are more literally true for Musorgsky than for many creative artists of his calibre and degree of genius. Why this should be so is itself a fascinating story, part of Russia's elaborate tradition of protecting, refashioning, and promoting the lives of her great cultural figures.

The life of Modest Musorgsky (1839–81) is exceptionally thin in events. Reliable information on his early years is scarce. He never married or established a home; for most of his adult life he did not have an address or residence of his own. His formal employment was of the most paltry kind. He never left the boundaries of Russia; in fact, his first extensive travel within the Russian Empire took place only two years before his death. Of his several ambitious works for the stage, only one was completed and performed during his lifetime. His "events" were his friends, his mentors, his encounters with ideas, his struggle for stable living arrangements, his dramatic and musical imagination.

Among Russian nineteenth-century biographies, Musorgsky's is one of the more difficult to tell. In instructive contrast to it, we might consider the lives of Leo Tolstoy (1828–1910) and Fyodor Dostoevsky (1821–81). These two great contemporaries, Russia's epic and dramatic realists in prose, are often compared with Musorgsky, "realist" musician and the chronicler of Russian history on stage. For the two novelists, documentation is terrifyingly thick. There is little we can say about Tolstoy that he did not say first, and better, about himself. Although the events of his life were not especially newsworthy, his personal letters and published diaries fill dozens of volumes; as a writer he excelled in the confessional mode, claiming ever higher levels of radical honesty toward his readers. He left a thick biological trace as well. Rooted in wealth, an ancestral estate, a wife and thirteen children, Tolstoy was a world industry in his own time. Dostoevsky's documentation was different, but equally part of a public cosmos. The sociopolitical crises of his time left a deep mark on his personal life: arrest, mock-death sentence and prison camp under one despotic tsar; imperial pardon, an engaged ideological life (and a tempestuous private one) culminating in glory during the reign of the next. Dying within weeks of Musorgsky in 1881, Dostoevsky – novelist, journalist, prophet – was an international celebrity.

Musorgsky's life is cast more in the mold of Nikolai Gogol (1809–1852). The life span of both men was just over forty years, and it had the same shrouded beginnings, brilliant but ambivalent core, and wretched end. Daily life in this mold was eventless, at times evasive, dependent for its sustenance upon a small, loyal circle of family or friends; it was the life of an unsettled bachelor, disjointed and for long periods unobserved. There were no memoirs, no extended confessions, no disciples – and increasingly, no secure means of support. In and out of health, Musorgsky would battle his demons with a show of bravado but, when pressed by his friends, was not inclined to divulge details. Like Gogol, he was an actor and mimic of genius, a master at reproducing intonation; again like Gogol, he was unwilling to explain himself or his art to others except by analogy and hyperbole. Being so isolated, however, he was deeply needful of the support of his mentors. His letters (epistolary art of the highest quality) are often masks.

Although we do not know if Musorgsky's creations were valued by Dostoevsky (whose musical tastes tended toward Glinka and the urban romance), evidence suggests that Musorgsky and Dostoevsky met at least once (in April 1879); in early February 1881, the composer attended a memorial evening for the deceased novelist, where he improvised keyboard variations on the funeral bells from the death of Boris.[1] Tolstoy, a competent pianist and passionately opinionated about music, became famous for his attacks on Beethoven and Wagner – but left no opinion of his compatriot. In 1901, the aging Tolstoy hosted at his estate of Yasnaya Polyana the Russian-French

1 Maria Olenina-d'Alheim (1869–1970)

singer Maria Olenina-d'Alheim, who was by that time spreading Musorgsky's fame around Europe. She performed for him several of the realistic songs and then, in French, "The Fieldmarshal" from the cycle *Songs and Dances of Death*. "Why did I think Musorgsky was a bad composer?" Tolstoy exclaimed. "What we just heard was more than excellent!"[2] But there is also an anecdote (by way of Tolstoy's doctor, who had been present as a very young man at Musorgsky's deathbed) that Tolstoy dismissed the entire "Musorgsky question" with the remark that "he liked neither talented drunks nor drunken talents."[3] Thus rests the matter with these greatest of Musorgsky's realist brethren in the literary circles of his time.

But shifty retrograde Gogol, from an earlier generation, was one of Musorgsky's deep and abiding loves. The composer's first fully conceptualized opera project, in the late 1860s, was a setting of several scenes from Gogol's play *Marriage*, in which the bachelor protagonist escapes his bride at the penultimate moment by jumping out the window and disappearing down the street. Musorgsky's final (also unfinished) opera project, begun in the early 1870s, was based on Gogol's folk fantasy, *Sorochintsy Fair*. Like all of Gogol's Ukrainian tales, it is full of shrewish wives, hard drink, erotic preening, the cunning of the devil. Musorgsky attributed the appeal of its ribald plot to his need for comic relief from the grim historical tasks of *Khovanshchina*, composed alongside it. A glance at Gogol's own story, however (not the opera, with its thrilling dream "Night on Bald Mountain" and its upbeat ending on the twirling Cossack dance, the hopak), suggests that Musorgsky as a reader of literature sought out in his soulmate Gogol not just compatible ideology and artistic forms but also compatible life anxieties. In Gogol's *Sorochintsy Fair*, what passes for comedy is largely terror. The dancing is either possessed or macabre; in the hallucinatory wedding scene that ends the tale, old hags "are propelled by the sheer power of drink into a movement that was faintly human, like lifeless machines set in motion by a mechanic, their intoxicated heads gently wagging." (Dancing as mesmerization and horror will govern the far more threatening *Songs and Dances of*

2 Poster announcing Olenina-d'Alheim's all-Musorgsky concert, 1902

Death as well.) First love in Gogol's story is a narcissistic cartoon; communication is carnival-abusive. The closing paragraph is a lament on the fading-out of all music into echo and from there into absolute silence. "How dreary it is," Gogol writes, "for the one left behind!"[4]

The point to emphasize, as we consider the literature that Musorgsky found real and worthy of musical transposition, is how much of Gogol "raw" speaks to the biography of the composer. Life thins out the more we live it. Death is increasingly in evidence; thus the pinning down and defining of death is always a more urgent task than the creation of new life. Gogol, even in his comedic guise, prefers the

voided stage and quiet curtain. From *Marriage* through the holy fool
alone on stage at the end of *Boris Godunov* to the mass suicide in Act 5
of *Khovanshchina*, this waning of life over time will become a
Musorgskian trademark. Gogol and Musorgsky resist the biographer.
Their life experience (or at least large stretches of it) was not something they wished to share, to commemorate, perhaps even to confront. Unlike Dostoevsky and Tolstoy, who set up their lives as
exemplary and drew often on their own experience, Musorgsky and
Gogol reincarnated themselves in the mouths, minds, and bodies of
others.

Thus on several planes Musorgsky is a recalcitrant subject. The
paucity of documents and adventures complements the composer's
own desire to evade close scrutiny. And as most music-lovers know, at
the level of the compositions themselves there is also colossal confusion. Much was apparently thought out by the composer but not written down; many pieces were left unfinished or unorchestrated,
in multiple versions, some retroactively redated. The whole of
Musorgsky's corpus was then subject to earnest, massive, posthumous "editing" (or better, rewriting) by Nikolai Rimsky-Korsakov,
who was eager that the work of his deceased friend not disappear
from the world stage unsung, together with its creator. Confused as
this story is, however, the Russian nineteenth century does offer some
relevant biographical models.

The major event of the second half of that century, the emancipation of the serfs and other social reforms of 1861–63, occurred at the
precise epicenter of Musorgsky's brief life. Viewed around that axis,
the composer's life might even be seen as "typical" for its age, reflecting gross national watersheds and displacements. Its first half was
routine for young men of his rank and means up through the mid-
1850s: childhood on a sleepy rural estate with the pleasures of nature,
a nanny, private tutors, and music teachers. Then came Cadet School
and the dissipated life of an officer of the Guards in St. Petersburg; the
presumption thereafter was a sinecure commission or early retire-
ment. A gentleman-composer like Mikhail Glinka (1804–57), with

income to travel or study abroad and the leisure to make music at home, was a natural result of such beginnings. But like most gentlemen of his generation, Musorgsky had a bifurcated life. The Emancipation Proclamation of March 1861, under the new tsar Alexander II, was a move of much daring and complexity that opened the way for viable Russian civic culture as surely as it ruined rural landowners of Musorgsky's sort. The reform program established local government, a legal system, a less brutal and more efficient army, relief from the more moronic forms of censorship: in short, a social and governmental structure that, although far from perfect, was at least worth taking seriously. Within the space of a few years, the creative intelligentsia – muzzled during the final decades of Tsar Nicholas I's rule – was revived. And the loss of income he suffered due to the Emancipation qualified Musorgsky, in the second half of his life, for a new prototypical biography, this time as a member of the "thinking intelligentsia" as it was defined in the 1860s–70s. The model was no longer the cosmopolitan gentleman-composer on his estate, but the impoverished nobleman turned bureaucrat or radical commune-dweller in the city, committed to seeking national forms of art. Musorgsky, it should be noted, never complained of any injustice done him in his reduced economic circumstances.

Beyond this point, paradigms cease to matter. Musorgsky was highly intellectual, impressionable, stubborn, lonely, and (after 1861) poor. He was also, of course, a musical genius – although of a peculiar sort, one who had literally no language in which to describe his experiments (Russian music theory barely existed in Russian, so even those radical composers who wished to explain their technique had to do so using German categories).[5] Given his temperamental bias against institutions and "official schools" of every type, and considering his reluctance to explain himself or to push his ideas on those who treated him kindly, he had few public forums where he might persuade (or train) others to hear things his way. Each of these traits contributes to the shape of his mature biography under the new and unsettled conditions that began in the 1860s.

Russian life suddenly had a large number of untested variables. There was the newly legitimated *narod* or "common people," a peasantry that had been raised almost overnight from the status of mere property to a rudimentary sort of citizenship. From the perspective of the upper classes, the *narod* was still largely mute – and needed to be given literary, philosophical, and musical expression. It had become legal to read a much wider press, to gather together in unsupervised groups, to experiment in unapproved genres, to become a professional in fields that earlier had belonged to foreigners or had carried no official recognition at home. As we shall see in chapter 3, Russia's first music schools were founded in the very heat of the Reform years, and the concept of professionalism became itself an object of controversy. During the reign of Nicholas I (1825–55), Russian patriotism had been summed up in the pious triad "Orthodoxy, Autocracy, Nationhood." Now, under Alexander II, in this precious and short-lived wedge of glasnost (the word takes on its emancipatory aura during this decade), many voices could compete.

In this debate, Musorgsky's voice was muffled, not of the mainstream. Even within the Balakirev Circle of gifted amateurs, he was an outsider. Of the two major camps that had been dispensing advice to cultured Russians since the 1840s, the so-called "Westernizers" and "Slavophiles," Musorgsky endorsed neither. Although he absorbed a very great deal from his Western peers, one could not call him a Westernizer. In his attacks on conservatory training, his enthusiasm for folk songs, his use of themes and texts from Russian history and literature for his operas, and his passion for setting to music the intonations of Russian speech, Musorgsky was fueled by a desire to free Russian national expression (as he put it in a letter in 1870) from the "high-heel inserts and tight shoes" forced upon it by European forms, thereby showing Russia as she was, in "bast sandals" (L, 145). Yet he was also no Slavophile, at least not in the sense current during the 1860s–70s. During those years, Slavophilism was rapidly taking on sentimental, pan-Slav, and imperial overtones (Dostoevsky, for example, endorsed all three trends with gusto). If the bleak endings

3 Portrait of Musorgsky by S. Aleksandrovskii, late 1870s

of Musorgsky's two historical operas are any index, however, the composer had a very different, very pessimistic view of the workings of historical time. He did not believe in Russia's divine (or imperial) mission. In fact, there is little evidence that he believed in any divinity at all. It is true that he believed in the Russian people – but not necessarily in their virtues, only in their distinctiveness and their energy. On balance, Musorgsky was not one to idealize human relations in any realm, which is surely one reason why his musical output is so undistinguished in its treatment of love. His aesthetic credo was not romantic, nor classical, nor (in any of the currencies of his time) "politically correct." He intended it only to be scrupulously scientific. What *was* Musorgsky's credo, stripped to its most basic form?

The question is not easily answered, for the composer rarely spoke plainly about his beliefs – about as rarely as he talked shop about his technique. But in one instance, a year before his death, Musorgsky did present himself straight, as he wished posterity to see him. In 1880, Hugo Riemann invited him to submit a brief autobiography for his *Musiklexikon*. The composer left several drafts of such a statement, in the third person, laundering the facts somewhat and stressing his non-identity with all other musical trends. For the biographer it is an unnerving document, for much in Musorgsky's evolution as a composer cannot be squared with it. Nevertheless, it does provide us with a glimpse of those priorities the composer had come to feel were most untranslatable and valuable in his own musical self. "Musorgsky cannot be classed with any existing group of musicians," he wrote, "either by the character of his compositions or by his musical views. The formula of his artistic *profession de foi* may be explained by his view, as a composer, of the task of art: art is a means for conversing with people, not an aim in itself. This guiding principle has defined the whole of his creative activity" (L, 419).

A major theme of this biography will be to consider what Musorgsky might have meant by that much quoted phrase *iskusstvo est' sredstvo dlia besedy s liud'mi* – "art is a means for conversing with people." This credo also affected aspects of his life other than the aesthetic: his letter-writing, his intensely creative bondings (most often with poets, artists, or other musicians), his preference for vocal and dramatic music over the purely instrumental or symphonic, his extraordinary gift for performing his own vocal compositions, especially while seated at the piano; his grasp of the role music can play in prolonging life and in coming to terms with death. We might end this preface with a series of questions that radiate outward from this quotation, illuminating many problematic nodes in Musorgsky's life. Although answers were not found for them all, such questions structured the nature of his personal as well as his musical quest.

What is an artistic (or more strictly, a musical) conversation? Are there laws governing its utterances and interactions? In the temporal arts, is the feel of open, receptive conversation necessarily opposed to formal structure? Need it conflict with the more fixed, heightened demands of theatricality? Musorgsky pulled back from the stricter forms of what he called *opéra dialogué* because in most people's minds, that mode of writing for the stage was associated solely with comedy – and he wished his plots to move forward with *serious*, even tragic, intonationally accurate recitative. But in music drama, can the "conversational," prosaic element be divorced from the realm of the low, trivial, and transient? Finally, if the artist is a "realist," must the conversation he or she sets up have referents in the outside world and be answerable to that world in some responsible and functional way, or can it too exist "for its own sake" (even if not as a musically-autonomous "aim in itself"), as some people say art must always exist?

Such questions were much discussed by progressive Russian musicians (and, in their own medium, by visual artists) during the 1860s. As Musorgsky's personal credo, however, "art as a means of conversation with people" is by no means clear and covers several unrelated concerns. Least problematic are the conversations – in the sense of dialogic and dramatic confrontations – that a musician sets up between personalities within a musical work, together with the whole realm of "program music" where Musorgsky's gifts were always strong. More difficult to assess is the role played by live mentors and audiences, especially in the case of a composer whose "school" is a tightly bonded group of like-minded composers which tutored itself by making, creating, and criticizing music in each other's homes. Without a doubt Musorgsky greatly prized the "communion" that took place during these musical evenings, which for over a decade were the cradle of his musical compositions, a place where he could perform his work (or supervise its performance) exactly as he envisioned it. Musorgsky, who bore solitude poorly, was deeply needful of human company and the reinforcement of loyal friends. But however he craved this social context, the record of his compositions suggests that he was not especially open, needful, or dependent upon other people for specific musical advice. His creative life was a conversation with himself.

1 Childhood and youth, 1839–1856

Modest Petrovich Musorgsky was born into an ancient gentry family in Karevo, Pskov province, on 9 March 1839, the fourth son of Pyotr Alexeyevich Musirskoy and his wife Yulia Ivanovna, née Chirikova. Legends and superstitions came to surround this event, and in general the precarious act of physical survival within the family. In 1832 the couple had lost their first son, Alexei, at the age of two, to a local epidemic (probably of smallpox); a second son, also called Alexei, was born a year later and he too died of the same disease, also under two years of age, in 1835. When Yulia Ivanovna gave birth to a third son in 1836, there was some talk of naming him again Alexei – Pyotr Alexeyevich, himself an only son, very much wished to honor his father in this traditional way – but that decision was overridden in favor of Filaret, a somewhat unusual Russian name. Some years later, Yulia Ivanovna began to call her elder son openly by his baptismal name, "Evgeny," usually kept private and known only to parents and godparents. Biographers have since surmised that the couple's use of these less common names and double-names was supposed to "deceive death," which had known all too readily where to look for an Alexei.

Children born into the Russian Orthodox faith are baptized after one of the saints or martyrs associated with their birth day; this venerable figure then becomes their patron and protector. A fourth son was born to the Musirskoys in 1839, on a day (9 March) that yielded up many sanctioned names, including such standard fare as Alexander, Ilya, and Nikolai. But again an unusual, out-of-the-way name was chosen: "Modest," from a Latin root meaning unassuming, humble, he who lies low. As one commentator has suggested, "The mother did not wish to select one of the names of the martyrs – in order to protect her child, to conceal him, if only by the semantics of his name, from the glance of fate that had carried off two of her children in their infancy."[1] The two surviving brothers were raised as precious, even as miraculous, escapees from the ordinary route, which was death.

How to celebrate the survival of children and how to deceive, appease, commemorate, and honor the fact of death: for the composer, these themes were to become very productive both dramatically and musically, filling the place that in other composers of his century was taken up by romantic love. The idea of children learning how to give the slip to Death hovers as an anxious shadow over the prehistory and early life of Modest Petrovich. In the 1870s, these themes would give rise to a piano suite, *Pictures from an Exhibition*, composed in despair over the death of a close friend, and to two song cycles, *The Nursery* and *Songs and Dances of Death*, unmatched in the annals of vocal music. The topic surfaces near the end of Musorgsky's life in a multitude of tiny, accidentally surviving details. In an epigraph, for example, written on the blank title-page of a blank music manuscript in 1880 – a year of destitution, humiliation, chronic alcoholism, and self-deception: "In the name of Alexander Sergeevich Pushkin," Musorgsky jotted down, "Neither glory, nor title, nor talent, nor power – nothing can save you; fate has so decreed!"[2] (The lines are Marfa's from the soothsaying scene in *Khovanshchina*; the plot is the exile and divestment of Prince Golitsyn's ancient house as part of Peter the Great's gradual elimination of Old Muscovy.) The Musorgsky lineage was likewise ancient, although it had never been numerous; in each generation several would survive but more would be cut down. It became extinct in 1984 with the passing of Filaret's granddaughter Tatiana Georgievna Musorgskaya, who died childless, the last to bear the family name.

Material on Musorgsky's early life is scanty. The most straightforward matters have been mystified (for example, the composer himself always gave his birthdate as 16 March, whereas it is actually 9 March), and to this day, debates continue over the correct spelling and pronunciation of the family name. There were irregularities in the Musorgsky family tree. The composer's father, Pyotr, was born out of wedlock, the son of an enserfed peasant woman by her gentry master, and legitimized only when he was already fully grown. How did this fact affect the way he viewed himself, his progeny, and their prospects in the world? What special anxieties or ambitions might he have passed on to his sons? (Not surprisingly, Soviet-era accounts of Musorgsky's life elevate the importance of this "peasant grandmother" to stellar heights, crediting her commoner's blood for everything from Musorgsky's perfect Russian ear to his dislike of Western musical practices.) And finally there is Musorgsky's own fondness for cover-up and masks – especially around beloved objects – which makes any reconstruction, even that of an obviously happy childhood, a risky enterprise. Nadezhda Purgold, long an intimate of the nationalist composers and later Rimsky-Korsakov's wife, wrote in her memoirs that "Musorgsky was an enemy of the routine or the prosaic, not only in music but in all aspects of life, even in minor details. Simple, ordinary words repelled him. He even managed to change and mangle surnames . . ." (MR, 36). Again evasion; again, slipping out from under the eye of fate. This lack of documentation and network of myths has been confronted in various ways by his biographers.

The first in this role was Vladimir Stasov (1824–1906), art critic, eminent functionary in the St. Petersburg Imperial Libraries, and indefatigable propagandist for Realism in Russian music. He befriended Musorgsky early and remained a precious, if possessive and opinionated, source of support through very difficult years. (In the 1870s, Musorgsky began to address him in letters as *généralissime*.) Two weeks after the composer's death, Stasov was already penning his first biographical sketch – a tendentious image that was to hold sway for a century. Not much competed with it. Musicologists in search of lore and local records did not begin to make field trips to Musorgsky's native Pskov region, 250 miles southwest of St. Petersburg, until the early twentieth century, long after all eyewitnesses had passed on. The first full genealogy for the family was compiled only in 1917.

Soviet scholarship culminated in a massive (although not uncensored) chronicle entitled *Musorgsky's Works and Days*, a "biography in documents" published in 1963. Out of its 600 pages, only seven are devoted to young Modest's first fifteen years. Most of the material assembled for the early years are retrospective accounts recalled (or constructed) from a great distance: unreliable recollections of a classmate ten years Musorgsky's junior, two casual pages by Filaret commissioned by Stasov in 1881, which omit all mention of growing up in Karevo; the composer's own quasi-fictionalized handful of paragraphs for the *Musiklexikon*, drafted in 1880, a year before his death. "What do we know about Musorgsky's childhood – the time when the personality of the artist-musician was being shaped and formed?" asks the editor Alexandra Orlova. "Almost nothing at all."[3]

By the 1980s, new methodologies on this slender information base were being tried out by Russian biographers. One result was a curious 700-page study of the composer's life by Roald Dobrovensky entitled *The Poor Knight: a Book About Musorgsky*, published in Riga in 1986.[4] It supplements early gaps in the biography with fictionalized episodes labeled "TK" (Russian initials for *tumannye kartiny*, "misty pictures"): scenes and dialogues that might have occurred but could not be documented. More in the scholarly vein is the sleuthing work of Nikolai Novikov, who in 1989 published a popular volume on the composer's formative years entitled *At the Source of Great Music*.[5] Novikov is a *kraeved* – that is, an ethnographer who specializes in a particular region [*krai*], its topography, its local records – and not a biographer. Whereas most biographers work from the top down, after the famous personality has already emerged and left a unique mark, a *kraeved* accumulates data from the bottom up, from the general unrecorded or routinely recorded life of a region, its patterns and statistical likelihoods. Ideally, then, the *kraeved* operates the way real time operates, not knowing in advance which infant will later be famous or which trinket will come to have biographical value. He or she begins by examining all existing "documents" (official records, geography, folklore) without any special brief for the biographical subject – and then assumes, in those cases where documentation for a particular family or event is absent, that the ordinary probably occurred. Although Novikov also admires his subject, acts the detective, and devises hypotheses, he does not go the route of "misty pictures." And he succeeds in clearing up a number of misconceptions simply by de-sensationalizing events and putting them in a broader social context. This chapter will take the "ethnographic" corrective into account when retelling Musorgsky's early years. Optimally, inconsistent memoirs can be brought into balance with the best stories still intact.

The Musorgsky genealogy can be traced back to Riurik, Viking founder of Novgorod in the ninth century. In family records the name is spelled a half-dozen ways (Muserskoy, Musarsky, Muserskoy, Musursky); the composer was registered at birth as a "Musirskoy." The elusive "g" appeared only in 1863, apparently on Filaret's initiative, and his brother inconsistently adopted it. (At the root of the family name is the lexeme *musor*, Russian word for garbage, an epithet believed to have been attached to a foul-mouthed ancestor in the fifteenth century. With the "g" added, a more seemly etymology becomes possible from the Greek *musurga*, meaning artist or musician.) There is still controversy over pronunciation. Should the accent fall on the second syllable, "in the Polish fashion," which Filaret preferred and which tended to muffle the unseemly root, or on the first syllable, technically correct in Russian and the usage endorsed by the composer for most of his adult life, despite (or perhaps because of) its degraded resonance?[6] Musorgsky made sport with the *musor* root in his signatures and self-epithets, signing his letters "Musinka" or "Musoryanin" [garbage-dweller]. Such caprice with names and "humble origins" was part of his talent for masking. Filaret, by far the more humorless aristocrat, did not share his brother's playfulness.

This detail too has implications for the elusive psyche of our subject. The composer's correspondence overwhelmingly supports the view that he considered himself none the less a nobleman for these low patches in his otherwise distinguished lineage (the "foul-mouthed" ancestor, the serf grandmother, the tardily legitimized father). He felt no more demeaned than Alexander Pushkin (whose great-grandfather, a black Abyssinian, was brought as a curio to the court of Peter the Great) had felt diminished by his exotic genealogy. Quite the contrary: genuine aristocrats, he surely divined, take offense at nothing, can absorb anything, and are always inclusionary and inventive rather than exclusionary. The tact with which Musorgsky accepted criticism, his skill at deflecting it, his gratitude for the support of others combined with his occasional shocking crudeness against abstract ideological foes, and, most of all, his unwillingness to obey his mentors when bounds were overstepped: these were aristocratic traits that Stasov, Balakirev, and others with a stake in Musorgsky's development could only read as weakness or stubbornness. On occasion these traits were read (as in one famous exchange of letters between those two exasperated mentors in 1863 over their twenty-three-year-old mutual friend) as "idiotism." Musorgsky did not delude himself about these incongruities. "I am discovering something in myself that is already obvious – a kind of looseness, a softness," he wrote with excruciating openness to Milii Balakirev on 11 March 1862. "You called it *doughiness*, I now recall, and I was a little hurt, because dough has the quality of retaining the impression of dirty fingers as well as clean ones. – However, I intend to get rid of this softness, it knocks me out" (L, 39).

As posterity has since confirmed, this root "idiocy" – or idiosyncrasy, singularity – of Musorgsky's nature was not at all that of a holy fool or village idiot. That image, so often and carelessly attributed to the composer, is one more passive projection back onto the creator of his own creations and masks. More likely, the composer's contrariness (which, according to Mme. Rimsky-Korsakov, could not abide the merely "routine and prosaic") was yet another attempt on his part to break free from that menu of received, restricted options that could easily seem, but in fact did not have to be, inevitable: in the functional harmony of his time, in the fate of his two elder siblings, in the very shape of Russia's destiny. Along some matrix the composer alone could map, a way out would be found. But could art be a "means for conversing with people" if this difficult task – providing some freedom of movement where everyone else saw and heard the hand of fate – was at the core of the conversation? Can a source for these quests be found in the formative years?

Stasov reports very little about Musorgsky's childhood, beyond vague mention of a German woman in Karevo who taught him music. No reminiscences have survived from Filaret Petrovich. Filaret's granddaughter Tatiana Georgievna did not have much early lore to relate, but she did remark that the older generation – her parents and grandparents – believed "a child should grow up surrounded by children" and that the Musorgsky youngsters, "according to family tradition, always played with the peasant children." Modest Petrovich himself gives us a bit more. In the opening of his *Musiklexicon* "autobiography" for this early period we read:

> Son of an ancient Russian family. Under the direct influence of his nurse, he became familiar with Russian fairy tales. The acquaintance with the spirit of folk-life was the main impulse of musical improvisations before he had learned even the rudimentary rules of piano-playing. His mother gave him his first piano lessons and he made such progress that at the age of seven he was playing small pieces by Liszt, and at nine played a grand concerto by [John] Field before a large audience at his parents' house. His father, who worshipped music, decided to develop the child's ability – and entrusted his further musical education to An. Herke in St. Petersburg (L, 416–17).

Thus ends Musorgsky's own account of his childhood, oriented wholly around the emergence of a precocious musical performer. Instead of siblings, hobbies, local legends, family history, the effects of the natural terrain, we have, in pride of place, the piano – the instrument of the youthful Musorgsky's first "conversations." Whatever the young boy heard, he could improvise upon; whatever else his parents meant to him during these years, most of all he wished posterity to know that they taught him to play. Although music training was routine for gentry families, still, it is of some interest that becoming a piano prodigy was perceived by the adult composer as the prime achievement of his childhood. Having a piano conveniently at hand was the major concern of his teenage years, the first piece of equipment his parents hurried to provide. All memoirists, even the most sour, note Modest Petrovich's astonishing skill at the keyboard – a skill that remained impeccably in place throughout the composer's physical decline.

Let us leave the practice room and move outside. What, in the 1840s, did this young piano prodigy see and hear in his daily rounds? Here the slow, vegetative pace of change across the Russian landscape genuinely benefits the biographer. In few Westernized nations have local vistas or whole horizons remained roughly the same from the eighteenth to the twentieth century. In Russia today, however, one can still visit Pushkin's rural estates and more or less "see what he saw"; such is also the case with Musorgsky's native region, as confirmed by singers and musicologists visiting in the 1980s. "No, here you won't exclaim, 'how beautiful!'" remarked Svetlana Vinogradova, a musicologist who had been working in the area for over a decade, after one of the centenary concerts in Karevo.

> Take a look around, there's simply nothing to fix your eye on: everything that could arouse hope, cause joy, caress the senses – it's all excluded. In nature like this there is a subtle, penetrating sense of sadness, like the face of the Mother of God on the old ikons – ascetic, tear-washed. This lake, shore, forest, the distant little villages look exactly like the gray sky, bright colors aren't appropriate here – and the artist must command a most subtle line in these places, just like the sound-palette of Musorgsky.[7]

In this colorless expanse of the rural Pskov landscape, the significant family story begins in 1828, with the marriage of Pyotr

Alexeyevich Musirskoy, age thirty, to Yulia Ivanovna Chirikova, the twenty-year-old daughter of a prosperous landlord from Naumovo (also an ancient family, with possibly a Mongolian ancestor). The bride was the fifth of eight children in a close-knit family of six daughters and two sons. They lost their mother early; from the age of seven, Yulia was raised by her elder siblings while she acted as nanny for the three youngest. Her upbringing was the customary one for well-to-do rural gentry girls. Its diverse routine included music, weaving and sewing lessons, and excellent training in two foreign languages (according to the family records, half the household income was spent on music and books).[8] The Chirikov manor house, high on a hill overlooking a lake, was a spacious structure with mezzanine and white columns. From its top stories, another thinly populated hill was visible about a mile away, beyond the church lands and cemetery: the village of Karevo.

Pyotr Alexeyevich's story of growing up in Karevo was quite different from that of his bride across the valley. Very few details are concretely known. He was probably born in 1798; in local books he is registered only as Pyotr, illegitimate son of the "house serf-maiden Irina." After three years, a patronymic was found for the little boy when his mother was formally married to the house serf Lev Parfyonov. This husband was not fictive (Irina gave birth to a second son, Avraam, who was raised as a serf); within three years, however, Parfyonov died. At that point the patronymic of the first-born Pyotr reverted to "Bogdanovich" [gift of God] – even though everyone in the village knew that his biological father was the Karevo landlord, Alexei Grigorievich Musirskoy, an officer with the rank of major in the Preobrazhensky Guards. Alexei Grigorievich did not hide his paternity. After the "orphaning," he installed the boy (along with his mother, one can presume) in the main house, arranging for him to be tutored as a *barchuk* (little *barin* or nobleman). In 1807, having inherited his elder brother's neighboring lands, Alexei Grigorievich moved to the new property with Irina and her four children (two "gentry" daughters had been born to her since her legal husband's death). But as late as 1817 the major was still registered as a bachelor. Even with the inheritance, it took some scrimping to send the boy to a St. Petersburg *gymnasium*. As Russian nobility, the Musirskoy clan was middling poor.

Pyotr Alexeyevich began to serve at a low-ranking job in the St. Petersburg Senate in 1814, at age sixteen. After six years of assiduous work he had achieved the rank of provincial secretary. During his service in the capital, two events of enormous importance occurred: in 1818 his father, age sixty, was officially married to the "serf-maiden" Irina Egorova; two years later, the Senate legitimized her four children. The "newlyweds" lived together another eight years, until the husband's death in 1826. One can only imagine Pyotr's relief, at age twenty-two, when his greatly delayed "rebirth" from peasant into nobleman at last came to pass. Without it, he was not a legal subject of the Empire and claims to his father's property were problematic. Only now could he consider marriage himself.

The Musirskoy holdings were impoverished and small compared with the Chirikov lands. Therefore, when Pyotr married in 1828, the couple settled on the wife's estate in Naumovo. It was there that the first two Alexeis were born, and died. In 1836, during the third pregnancy, understandably desperate to leave the site of those two tiny identical graves, the Musirskoys moved to Karevo. While he was alive, Alexei Grigorievich, Pyotr's father, had always done well by Irina's extended peasant family, welcoming them as members of the household. Now the widowed Irina (with her patronymic upgraded from Egorovna to the more genteel "Georgievna") followed her son Pyotr and his wife to the new residence.

The Karevo homestead was smaller and poorer than Naumovo. It more readily provided that balance between unvarnished peasant life and high-cultural aspirations (language lessons, a piano) that the couple's fourth son Modest, born three years later, was to recall with such gratitude. In the Karevo context, the claim of the composer's grand-niece Tatiana Georgievna that "by family tradition" the Musorgsky youngsters "always played with the peasant children" makes perfect sense. For they were, in effect, relatives. But also fully understandable was the ardent desire on the part of Pyotr Alexeyevich – who had been legitimated and ennobled by a hair's breadth – to insure his surviving sons a place in the nobility, to enroll them in the Preobrazhensky Guards in which their grandfather had served, to make sure that for them the countryside was a leisurely option but not a dead-ended fate. As we shall see in the following chapter, all eyewitness accounts of Musorgsky as a young officer stress his foppishness, his immaculate dress, his lisping French and exquisite salon manner. There is no contradiction here between "childhood games with peasants" and (as Alexander Borodin described the aristocratic, seventeen-year-old officer Modest Petrovich in 1856) "a graceful little boy . . . his hair sleek and pomaded, his fingernails manicured, his carefully tended hands those of a gentleman" (L, 28). In serfholding Russia as in the slaveowning United States, the most intimate relations flourished between masters and the members of a servitor class without any confusion or close identification of one by the other. But one thing seems certain: that Irina Georgievna's continued presence in the household (she died in 1849, when Modest was ten years old), as both blood grandmother to the boys and as an illiterate, "nanny"-like bridge to the Musirskoy serfs, must have brought her two well-educated grandsons into unusually close contact with local folklore and its rituals.

Let us now consider this second dominant feature of Musorgsky's childhood, after mastery of the piano, that he singled out in his autobiographical sketch: "fairytales and the spirit of folk-life." The Karevo lands, for all their natural abundance of forests, lakes, and marshes, were more poor than prosperous. Ethnographers and *kraevedy* who have studied the region's folklore – and local folk forms are always closely tied to economic reality – testify to "the thinness of the soil, weather conditions that were often unpropitious, the low level of harvests, and, as a result, the dominant fact of poverty among the peasants."[9] Novikov remarks that the village of Karevo in particular was known throughout the region as a "haven for widows with children";

apparently, families without breadwinners could expect to find charity there and meager subsistence. One must not confuse a Russian "gentry homestead" with an "estate," an English manor house, or a thriving agricultural enterprise in the New World. In prerevolutionary Russia, ancient aristocratic names could be found on miserable plots, working the soil alongside a small number of their own serfs. The middling rural gentry in this region – indeed, in most of Russia – lived in modest wooden houses, substantial only when compared to the shabbiness of the surrounding peasant huts; the sum of domestics (that is, house serfs, of which the Musirskoys in Karevo had over a dozen) was no indication of elegance or wealth. Idle hangers-on and superfluous servants were a sign of stagnation and inefficiency.

The richness of the region must be sought not in its economic prosperity but in its folk tradition. Here, too, the Russian *kraeved* enjoys an advantage over professional counterparts in more Westernized lands, because Russian peasant culture, like the local horizon of the isolated village, has been tenacious and slow to change. Songs recorded on the first wax cylinders by pioneering Russian ethnomusicologists in the late 1890s could well have been what the young Modest and his brother heard daily in the 1840s. Most elaborate in the region were calendar and wedding songs, *prichitaniia* or ritual lamentations (specialized for weddings, funerals, and the military recruitment season), and then, for middle-aged and elderly women, the "lament with a cuckoo" [*plach s kukushkoi*], an outpouring of human grief sung together with nature's traditional bird of sadness. The region, it appears, was a goldmine of laments. Folklorists inform us that the local manner of performance favored a strongly marked melodic line, extreme intonational expressivity, uneven and exacerbated rhythms, maximally short breathing periods for the phrase, abrupt drops of the voice to the lower registers, often in the middle of a word – in brief, rigorously stylized musical communication.

These facts of local folk music are of some importance for understanding not only Musorgsky's later evolution as a composer, but also the reception, paraphrase, and propagation of his "theories" by friends and foes alike. In the mid-1860s, as we shall see, Musorgsky was seized by a passion for "reflecting Russian speech honestly in music." Inspired partly by early Romantic notions of musical expression and partly by the vocal placement of Russian women's folk singing (in the throat, with glottal ornamentation, rather than a more clarified "head voice"), he believed there was a continuum between talking and singing. He designed experiments to test the boundary: first, vocal "musicalizations" of children's conversations overheard in everyday life (the *Nursery* cycle) and then, on a larger scale, with a musical setting of Gogol's chopped and prosy dramatic dialogue in the short drama *Marriage*. Musorgsky began with the assumption that each person, in fact each separate utterance of each person, is subtly different. With practice, a composer could both discern this difference and formulate a unique aural expression for each context – that is, reproduce a conversation. Vladimir Stasov adored these naturalistic experiments. They were everything that "national" meant to him: untranslatably Russian, abrasive and artless in comparison with the rounded, imported *chanson* or *Lied*, and in their subject matter comic, prosaic, attractively vulgar. In part through Stasov's enthusiastic (if imprecise) writings on the topic, what Musorgsky was doing in the 1860s came to be identified with fidelity to the Russian people, to unfettered or untutored expression, and to folk forms.

But of all artistic production, "folk forms" are the least spontaneous, individuated, or free. As the laments from Karevo – and in fact all traditional peasant singing – demonstrate, such music and narrative are not constructed as outlets for the unique personal statement. Quite the contrary: in the interests of a stable community (and as psychological relief for the sufferer as well), the mourner is expected to adjust her grief to the stylized requirements of the song. The singer disciplines herself through form and dissolves her private needs in it. As the first gatherers of Russian folk song discovered, both solo and choral performances were subject to the same "self-effacing" logic: it was impossible to get an accurate transcription of isolated individual undervoices (*podgoloski*) one voice at a time, because heterophonic choral performance was a single unit that lacked easily separable strands. The musical style of the folk was communal and essentially emotionless. While in the act of singing, the folksinger was not a person, but a vessel.[10]

Vladimir Stasov, who invented the image of Musorgsky, Russian Realist, and championed declamatory musical prose, never grasped this incipient "neoclassicism" of folk culture. A quarter century after Musorgsky's death, in 1904, at age eighty, Stasov was still speaking rapturously of Russian nationalism in music as the inevitable disappearance of "convention and implausibility" and as the victory of "truth and naturalness." But the "realist-mimetic" attempt to make music conform to the expressive contour of Russian speech (which Musorgsky did pursue passionately in the mid-1860s) was not a folk-ish project. It was, as the composer insisted, an experiment in accurate individualized expression. Its inspiration was thoroughly Western, taken from Händel and German theorists of intonation with whom the precociously intellectual Musorgsky had become enamored in his late teens. Native folk culture, in contrast, was formulaic and collective. Both the setting of individual speech and the use of folk forms required from the artist an intuitive grasp of constraints, although of different sorts. Musorgsky did not consider his investigations into individualization to be exercises in freedom. In a letter to Stasov in the fall of 1872, he thrilled over Darwin – because that great British naturalist knew "exactly the kind of animal he has to deal with . . . without Man being aware of it, he is *gripped in a vise* . . . [however,] not only is Man's pride not torn from him by this violence, but sitting within Darwin's vise is even pleasant, to the point of bliss" (L, 198).

This sense of constriction and subsequent aesthetic heightening is what the young Modest must have absorbed from the peasant rituals that he encountered in Karevo. Folk expression does not celebrate the individual, any more than Darwin's genius focused on the single biological specimen. Folkloric form was a "vise": it confirmed one's helplessness in the face of fate. To reconcile oneself in a dignified way to this fate, and at the same time to use one's creativity and inventiveness to escape wherever possible from it: this was the key to survival.

Other, less morbid aspects of the surrounding musical culture surely also left their mark on the impressionable boy: folk festivities, work songs, the Russian Orthodox chants intoned in local Church services. Ethnographers emphasize the unusually high level of *pevuchest'* ["songfulness"] in the region, the fact that social messages were often sung rather than merely spoken. Every important social ritual was accompanied by "sung speech." Music here was not *added* to words; it was an indivisible part of the form and content of the verbal message from the start. Such a fused communicative unit, words plus pitch and rhythm, did indeed become part of Musorgsky's declamatory experiments. These tonally expressive genres had more individuating potential than the stylized "lament with a cuckoo," and were doubtless a more flexible part of that "spirit of folk-life" which the composer later recalled as a formative influence. His regular retreats home to the countryside, which continued into the late 1860s, were always restorative.

The above comments on peasant music culture – its points of liberation and its inherent constriction – also help to explain why Musorgsky, settled in the city and freshly orphaned in the mid-1860s, might have been experimenting precisely *against* the grain of "folk truth." In striving to give a personalized profile to every voice he heard, or to every departed voice he remembered with anguish and a sense of loss, he was trying to make that voice precisely *not* collective and generalizable. He strove to recapture a precious, singular lost image – his mother in the first instance, but the pattern of loss would be repeated. This exhilarating, if utopian, thread of hope could have been one animating motivation behind the "declamation experiments." Again we glimpse what is a leitmotif of this biography: Musorgsky seeking ways out of what he feared were dead-ended or entropic systems, the Musirskoy impulse to trick death.

In 1849, the year grandmother Irina died, Pyotr Alexeyevich took his two sons, aged thirteen and ten, to St. Petersburg. Filaret was not accepted into the family's first-choice school, for Sub-ensigns of the

4 Musorgsky as an ensign in the Cadet School, St. Petersburg
(sketch by M. Mikeshin)

Guard and Cavalry Junkers; but after some anxious moments, places were found for the two brothers in the Peterschule, a prestigious secondary school for sons of the gentry and minor nobility. They boarded with the school inspector, whose establishment, fortunately, was "musically equipped" (the keyboard improvisations of the ten-year-old newcomer astonished the German hosts). Modest began piano lessons with the admired and severe music pedagogue, Anton Herke. (Filaret too was a pupil, for a time.) The brothers had brought little by way of education from Karevo to the capital except piano-playing skills and fluency in French and German, thanks to their nannies and tutors. It served them well. The Peterschule was a German classical *gymnasium*, with instruction in that language and a thoroughly trilingual social life. Modest was completely at home in three languages within the year.

Herke, for his part, was delighted with his protégé. At the age of twelve, in a recital given at the home of a lady-in-waiting at court, little Modest so brilliantly performed a concert rondo that Herke presented him with a copy of the first Beethoven A♭ Sonata. In 1851, Modest took some further preparatory courses in military subjects, and the following year, when Modest was thirteen, the two brothers matriculated to the Cadet School of the Imperial Guards. For Filaret, Cadet School was pro forma. He would inherit responsibility for the bulk of the family lands and settle in its manor house. For Modest, the second son of a noble house, the military was a career.

Little of a personal nature is known about the four years (1852–56) that Modest spent at the Cadet School. There are schedules of summer encampments and drills, Filaret's brief reminiscences, and the unreliable, rumor-laced memoirs of the minor composer Nikolai Kompaneiskii (1848–1910), Musorgsky's junior by nine years and a pupil at the same school. "[My brother] was a very good student at the Cadet School," wrote Filaret (who was a much less bookish personality). "Always among the top ten ... he was an avid reader of history and enthusiastically read German philosophy" (MR, 26). At thirteen Modest produced his first musical composition, "Porte-enseigne Polka," dedicated to his classmates. In his final year of study (1856),

still unlearned in harmony or composition, the self-confident virtuoso even planned an opera after Victor Hugo's *Han d'Islande* (nothing
came of it). All the while, a great deal of piano-playing went on: music-
making at the director's home, improvisations at cadet dances. In retrospect, however, the most important question we must ask of this
relatively blank period is also the most delicate: was it here, trapped
with dissolute young officers in the fast lane, that the drinking began?

Kompaneiskii's memoirs, one of the few documents for this
period, have been heavily mined for insights into Musorgsky's adolescence. For several reasons, this is unfortunate. Kompaneiskii appears
to have hated the school – and, what is more, to have nurtured a professional musician's distrust of Musorgsky as composer along with a
Russian academic's inability to allow great artists to answer for their
own choices and vices. His memoir of the Cadet School is one long
story of oppressive drill, lackeydom, womanizing, drunkenness – all
of which, it seems, the director encouraged as befitting a dashing
young Russian officer. That Modest Petrovich, the young piano virtuoso with the fine light baritone voice, remained "utterly unaware of
the elementary rules of music" was a fact Kompaneiskii himself confirmed frequently; he also records that Musorgsky was wholly ignor-
ant of Russian composers and of Russian church music (even though
Musorgsky had claimed, in his autobiographical sketch, to have
"acquired a profound knowledge of its essence" through one Father
Krupsky, the regimental priest, a man who himself made no pretense
to deep knowledge of the subject). "Musorgsky mastered the external qualities of an officer of the Preobrazhensky [Guards],"
Kompaneiskii concludes.

> He even learned how to drink himself to oblivion; in addition, he
> abandoned his reprehensible studies of German philosophy . . . But
> he could not afford to spend as much money as his comrades did. He
> participated in the carousing, and for nights on end he would pound
> out polkas on the ivories. His comrades appreciated his services, but
> this was not sufficient to support the honor of the Guards' uniform.
> One had to spend one's fortune. (MR, 2)

5 Musorgsky as a young officer, 1856

Musorgsky did not have that fortune to squander – and so, according to the canonized scenario, in 1858, having achieved the rank of ensign, his health already impaired and his bad habits in place, he resigned from the service.

Stasov, in his reminiscences, recalls this pivotal moment. By the spring of 1858, the nineteen-year-old Musorgsky had been working on music seriously with his first mentor Milii Balakirev for over a year. "I diligently tried to talk him out of resigning," Stasov wrote in his memoirs. "I used to tell him that Lermontov himself was able to be an officer in the hussars and at the same time a great poet, in spite of the expenses and the parades. Musorgsky would reply: 'That was Lermontov, and I am not like him; maybe he was able to cope with it, but I cannot. Military service keeps me from working'" (MR, 8). This little exchange has everything. There is the sensible, if misplaced, advice of a concerned friend, who could hardly expect this dandy and dilettante to support himself on music alone; there is humility on the part of genius and commitment to the hard work of art; there is even a "progressive" hint (so appealing to later Soviet biographers) at the dissoluteness of service in the Imperial Guards. But mostly, the conversation suggests that the sensitive young ensign Modest Musorgsky – coddled in Karevo by his parents and then abandoned in the military barracks of St. Petersburg, Russia's Sodom – was helpless to resist its alien values and culture: he "could not cope." The martyrology had begun.

This familiar story should be adjusted. Novikov, the *kraeved* who examined local Karevo records for traces of its everyday village life, turned his attention to the St. Petersburg schooling and service years (1849–58) as well.[11] Checking out municipal archives and receipts, he confirmed his hunch that the two beloved Musirskoy sons would never have been "abandoned" in the city; every other year, Pyotr Alexeyevich (until his death in 1853) and Yulia Ivanovna rented quarters in St. Petersburg and moved there to live, while at other times there were always relatives on call for the two boys. In 1857, a Becker piano was installed in the apartment for Modest. Beginning in that year, it was the mother who paid Balakirev – and generously – for the music lessons (or better, music sessions) spent with her younger son. Once widowed, Yulia Ivanovna lived for long stretches in St. Petersburg; Balakirev knew her and her cooking well. To the extent they wished to avail themselves of it, the Musirskoy sons were still at home.

In short, a truer picture of Musorgsky's adolescence, preferable to the incipient martyrology, would seem to be this. A military officer's life was not to the young Modest's taste. Certainly it was a piece of bad luck that in Imperial Russia of the time, second sons were expected to take this route. But Modest was diligent, popular, fastidious in his duties, and – of crucial importance – sheltered from its worst aspects. Family presence remained strong. If, as officers, the brothers occasionally caroused, it was not because they had nowhere else to go. Unlike the poet Lermontov (1814–41, an artist in the rebellious Romantic-Byronic mode who died in a duel at age twenty-seven), Modest was never attracted by locker-room gossip or by the specifically male diversions of regimental life: horses, gambling, duels. He was not known to womanize at all. He was pampered, a creature of the salon, much more the performer than he was the competitor or pursuer. After his resignation from the service, the family became *more* present in his life, not less. As Filaret records matter-of-factly in his brief remarks about his brother, "during the years 1858 to 1863, he lived with different members of the family, until 1862 he lived with mother and me, and in the latter part of 1862 and 1863, with me and my wife" (MR, 27). What broke Musorgsky and triggered the first serious alcoholic interval, I think we must conclude, was not military drill, classes taught by martinets, or the pressure of mandatory drinking and whoring for the honor of the Guards. It was the death of his mother.

Yulia Ivanovna gave up the St. Petersburg residence and moved back to Karevo in 1863. She died at the rural manor two years later, in her mid-fifties, apparently of dropsy. We know that the months immediately following her death were deeply awful for her younger son.

And in the fall of 1865, what he called his "nervous disorder" surfaced for the first time so seriously that it could not be capped and hidden away. The composer's biographers have not, I believe, sufficiently appreciated the extent to which Musorgsky's subsequent pattern of creativity and collapse is tied precisely to the sorts of services his mother had provided, far into his adulthood.

"With the passage of years, [Musorgsky] did not grow apart from his female parent, as most people do, pursuing the interests of an independent life," Dobrovensky notes in his biography. "He never fully separated himself, never became autonomous."[12] The traits Musorgsky most valued in himself he attributed to her; thus he could not "outgrow" them without ceasing to grow altogether. In her memoirs of the composer, Glinka's sister Liudmila Shestakova recalls how often Modest Petrovich, when complimented on his social delicacy and self-control, would say: "for that I am indebted to my mother, she was a sacred woman" (MR, 53). Being orphaned affects every child differently. For Musorgsky, it was devastating; for this loss, he never forgave Death. Unmetered love, musical sensitivity, discreet financial support, regular meals, "the samovar never cold," a ready piano, perfect tact – and the sense, overall, of being organically at the center of another person's life: all this had become the young man's birthright. Without it, he was unhinged.

The year 1865 already exceeds the bounds of the present chapter. One further family detail must be mentioned, however, before we leave the adolescent period. This is the status of Filaret Petrovich. On two accounts, the older brother has been demonized in biographies of the composer. First, he was a self-conscious aristocrat who had the misfortune, we may now retroactively say, to include in his remarks on his younger sibling a few lines about Modest's love of the common people: my brother, Filaret observed, "considered the Russian peasant a real human being (in this he was sadly mistaken)." Soviet scholars, when not so offended by this impiety that they omit the phrase altogether (as was long the practice with Musorgsky's ugly anti-Semitic remarks), have felt obliged to react to it with horror. Such

6 Musorgsky (right) with his brother Filaret, 1858

aversion was all the more appropriate, because Filaret – so the canonized biography goes – had a second failing, material greed. Having
inherited all the family land and with wife and two children to support, he took advantage of his bachelor brother's generosity and, at
the time of the Emancipation, "managed" affairs so that Modest had
nothing. This rumor was reinforced by Musorgsky's close friend and

the most gifted singer of his songs, Aleksandra Molas (the one woman who pined long, hard, and fruitlessly for Modest Petrovich), when she recorded in her memoirs this face-saving but unsubstantiated sentiment: "I know that he gave his elder brother his father's estate, saying: 'My brother is married, he has children; as for me, I will never marry and I can make it on my own'" (MR, 110). Again, the comfortable story of genius deceived by the philistines; again, Musorgsky as martyr.

Novikov has looked into this "disinheritance myth" as well.[13] As his correspondence testifies, Modest remained on close terms with his brother (whom he called "Kitushka") and was indeed beholden to him. In 1861, Filaret agreed to take on the horrendous task of liberating the Karevo, Naumovo and Polutino serfs, together with land and according to a complex set of tax regulations. Filaret spared his sensitive, talented sibling this exhausting work, because "Modinka" had no head at all for such details; it was the sort of thing his mother always did for him. From Musorgsky's letters during 1862–63 we know that on occasion the composer had to remain in Karevo to clear up some aspect of the settlement, his brother being elsewhere engaged. Modest disliked this running about and understood little of what was at stake. Filaret did not cheat his brother. The composer remained the legal landlord of the remaining Karevo lands – but he had no idea how to get money out of them. In November 1876, badly in need of cash, Musorgsky wrote politely to his steward-tenant Alexander Morozov in Karevo to send "as much money as possible" and to let him know "how the farming arrangements are faring" (L, 350). The steward obviously felt under no obligation to comply.

Such details matter in the larger context, for there were several prototypes of the post-Emancipation Russian landlord, of which Modest Musorgsky's kindly, confused, unprofitable model was only one. Leo Tolstoy represented the most responsible and energetic type. Rich to begin with, Tolstoy returned home to Yasnaya Polyana in 1861, after army service and a stretch of city living, to devote himself full-time to reorganizing his estate, serving as Justice of the Peace in peasant arbitrations, and setting up peasant schools. His wealth remained intact. Turgenev, even wealthier, found excellent managers for his properties and moved abroad. Tchaikovsky, who had no family fortune and younger brothers to sponsor, did have fame, social connections, a conservatory post, and a devoted financial patron. Dostoevsky (who had little capital in any event) was a gambler and very bad with money, but he married a superb household manager and died free of debt. Musorgsky, like Gogol, had neither wife nor manager. He could be helped by his brother, but not forever, and not when his own native delicacy stood in the way.

At the end of the 1850s, Musorgsky was on the brink of a full-time musical life. Alexander Borodin, then a medical intern, first met him in the fall of 1856 (Musorgsky was the officer on duty at the hospital where Borodin was assigned). At soirées during that year, Borodin marveled at the young man's refined social behavior and at his "little closely-fitting uniform, as neat as a pin." "He had graceful and aristocratic manners," Borodin recalled, "his conversation, spoken slightly through his teeth and interspersed with French sentences, was somewhat artificial but nonetheless quite aristocratic. There was a hint of foppishness, although a very moderate one. He was unusually courteous and well brought up . . . He would sit down at the piano and, affectedly throwing up his hands, would begin to play, very sweetly, graciously, excerpts [from fashionable Italian opera] . . . while all around him, people were buzzing in a chorus: '*Charmant, délicieux!*'" (MR, 28).

Three years later, Borodin met Musorgsky again, this time in civilian dress. A new phase of his life had begun.

2 Apprenticeship in St. Petersburg, 1850s–1860s: composers' evenings and the commune

Memoirs are fickle and tricky to read. The verbal portrait that Alexander Borodin has left us of the fastidious, well manicured, seventeen-year-old "toy officer" Modest Petrovich, who delighted ladies in the salon with his piano improvisations and his lisping French, is as familiar to readers of his biography as Repin's pre-death portrait (slovenly genius representing the spirit of Russia) is familiar to the Western music-loving world. In his 1986 biography of the composer, Dobrovensky tried to free his subject of some of these more stereotyped myths. He reminds us of the obvious, that memoirs, by their very nature, tell us as much about the memoirist as about the subject. Borodin – himself the illegitimate son of a Georgian prince and sensitive to matters of rank – was by that time already a research chemist and working daily on cadavers. His own hands were scarred with disinfectants and acid; of course he noticed Modest Petrovich's aristocratically soft hands and perfect nails![1]

But Dobrovensky then points out what might be less obvious: that Borodin's account of the young Musorgsky, like most other surviving accounts, was composed many decades after the fact. The little piano-playing officer was hardly worth watching or remembering in 1856. The famous recollections we now have were commissioned by Stasov in 1881, urgently, in an attempt to pull together a composite image of his deceased friend before he disappeared into the grave. By that time, there was indeed great talent to commemorate – even if in Stasov's opinion it had long been in decline. In keeping with this image, Stasov sought out accounts that would emphasize the contrast between the composer's early promise and his ultimate collapse. Since information about Musorgsky's apprenticeship depends heavily upon memoirs, we should keep their retroactive nature fully in mind.

Borodin continues his memoir on Musorgsky with their second encounter three years later, in 1859. "He had matured considerably and had started to put on weight," Borodin writes.

> He no longer had an officer's mannerisms. He was still elegantly dressed, his manners were still refined, but that hint of foppishness had totally vanished . . . Then Musorgsky started to talk enthusiastically about Schumann's symphonies, which at the time were totally unknown to me. He started sketching in excerpts of Schumann's Symphony [No. 3] in E♭ major. When he reached the development section, he stopped playing and said: "Well, now musical mathematics begin." It was all new and very attractive to me . . . Only then did I learn that he also wrote music.

In a subsequent segment, Borodin describes their third meeting, after another three-year period, in 1862. Musorgsky and Balakirev were at the piano, rendering Rimsky-Korsakov's new symphony. "Musorgsky's playing was quite different from what I had heard during our first two meetings. I was dazzled by the brilliance, expressiveness, and energy of the performance, as well as by the beauty of the piece" (MR, 29–30). Borodin recalls being abashed and reluctant when Musorgsky politely asked to see some of his own compositions.

The transformation registered in these three equally spaced portraits – 1856, 1859, 1862 – constitutes an affirmative upswing, a hopeful stretch of years in the composer's life. By 1858, he was out of the military. He was still a landed proprietor of comfortable, if not lavish, means. One year previously, his mother had settled in St. Petersburg, in a roomy house on Grebetsky Street where she could attend full-time to the practical needs of her two sons. And Musorgsky, having decided to devote his life wholly to music at a time when he had little more than

7 Nikolai Rimsky-Korsakov (left)
   and Milii Balakirev (right)
   (sketches by Ilya Repin)

a pianistic acquaintance with it, was fortunate enough to find sympathy from a series of extraordinary musical acquaintances. The first phase of his emergence as a composer can be seen as intense, if idiosyncratic, musical study under a sequence of mentors – and his growing ability to resist their proffered guidance.

The story begins with the formation of the "Balakirev Circle," that group of gifted amateurs later known loosely to musical history as the Russian nationalist composers, "The Five," or the *Moguchaya kuchka* ("Mighty Little Heap"). In December 1857, the eighteen-year-old Musorgsky was introduced to Milii Balakirev. The meeting took place during a musical evening at the home of the composer Alexander Dargomyzhsky, friend of Mikhail Glinka (who had died that year in self-imposed exile in Berlin, disillusioned with Russia). For the young officer-pianist, who had scarcely suspected the existence of "Russian composers," it was a landmark event. Balakirev, a precocious, restless provincial with a wealthy patron, had met Glinka in St. Petersburg before the latter's departure for Europe; this mantle of legitimacy increased the young man's already formidable charisma. Balakirev combined spectacular practical musical skills (extensive conducting experience, wide musical repertory, superb aural memory, virtuosic piano skills, an intuitive gift for form) with a passion for teaching. Over the next few years, he put together a "study circle" that came to include a motley group of part-time musicians (members of the *kuchka*, thus called *kuchkisty*) scarcely out of their teens: César Cui, an army engineer; Alexander Borodin, an excellent chemist; Nikolai Rimsky-Korsakov, a naval officer; and (least promising of the lot, in his opinion) Modest Musorgsky, boy wonder at the keyboard, soon to be retired from the Imperial Guards. The "textbooks" for the circle were not formal lessons in harmony and counterpoint but piano duet reductions of the latest European music. In 1857, Balakirev was only twenty-one years old, yet from the start he was an authoritative mentor for the other, less experienced musicians.

For several years, "Balakirev evenings" took place regularly, usually on Saturday nights. Seated at the keyboard, these musicians-in-training would study and perform scores by Schumann, Berlioz, Lizst, Glinka, Dargomyzhsky. Then Balakirev would analyze and correct his "students'" compositions. Musorgsky was in a peculiar position at these sessions. On the one hand, he was an accomplished pianist and indispensable partner in practical music-making; on the other, his personality was so foppish, malleable, likeable, and his efforts at composition so juvenile and scattered, that it was hard to take him seriously. The *kuchkisty* exchanged lively, learned letters with one another on a regular basis, and Musorgsky's attempts at composition became a frequent butt of unkind criticism. An avuncular attitude evolved toward Modest Petrovich on the part of César Cui, who was all of four years older but by temperament infinitely more assertive and didactic. Musorgsky's letters to Cui lavish praise on the latter's compositions (mediocre overall), whereas Cui's comments to him tend to condescend. But it is Modest Petrovich's relationship and correspondence with Balakirev that dominates this apprenticeship period.

Musorgsky's letters to his mentor are poignant and at times even painful to read. They start in 1857, when the music sessions began (Balakirev, a poor man, supported himself by giving lessons) and taper off by the mid-1860s, a time of Balakirev's peak involvement in the musical life of the capital. It appears that this epistolary outlet was a mix of diary, confession, and homework assignment for the younger man. But for all the affectionate epithets ("Most precious Milii!") and brutally frank admissions in these letters, Modest remained on formal second-person-plural terms with Balakirev – as he did with almost all his musical contacts, including Rimsky-Korsakov, a very close friend, eventually a housemate, and five years his junior. This was apparently deliberate policy on the part of the *kuchkist* composers and their sponsor Stasov, for it lent an air of dignity to their transactions. With the "non-musicians" Golenishchev-Kutuzov, Nikolai Molas, and his later housemate Pavel Naumov, Musorgsky was on intimate forms of address.

Balakirev was absolutely frank about his qualifications as a teacher. In a rather cold memoir, culled together by Stasov in 1881, Balakirev noted that two decades earlier, he and the deceased had played "all of the musical repertoire that existed at that time" in piano duet versions, but, "since I had not been trained in music theory, I could not teach Musorgsky harmony . . . I could, however, explain the form of a composition . . . Since I was unable to explain the principles of voice leading to him, i.e. harmony, I simply made corrections here and there where I felt something was amiss" (MR, 31). Certainly the supreme self-confidence of this gifted autodidact-instructor must have inspired Musorgsky in general (if *he* is so convinced he is right, in the absence of textbooks and rules, then what is to prevent me?), even as it unnerved him in the particulars. Balakirev's "method" has been variously assessed by his own circle, and by history.

Understandably, Rimsky-Korsakov, who went on to become professor of composition and theory at the St. Petersburg Conservatory, was the harshest toward the method. In his autobiography he recalled the Balakirev evenings. "With all his native intelligence and brilliant abilities," Rimsky wrote,

> there was one thing [Balakirev] failed to understand: that what was good for him in the matter of musical education was of no use whatsoever for others . . . A composition was never considered as a whole in its aesthetic significance . . . A pupil like myself had to submit to Balakirev a proposed composition in its embryo, say, even the first four or eight bars. Balakirev would immediately make corrections, indicating how to recast such an embryo; he would criticize it, would praise and extol the first two bars, but would censure the next two, ridicule them, and try hard to make the author disgusted with them . . . [Since Balakirev] had acquired everything by his own astounding many-sided talent and experience quite without labor and without system, he had no idea of any systems . . . There was no need of training [he said]: one must begin to compose outright.[2]

Others – not surprisingly, Stasov's disciples – have been more generous, pointing out that Balakirev's policy of mastering musical composition through a close study of existing works was in fact quite progressive as pedagogy.[3] Musorgsky himself, highly sensitive to personal tone and needful his whole life of male bonding, seemed to thrive on such individualized attention. At least, his relationship with Balakirev assumed a decidedly intimate and confessional tone from the start. It would take Musorgsky a decade to outgrow it.

Several letters will illustrate the progression of this vital, but eventually enervating, relationship. The first is from February 1860. Musorgsky had just celebrated his debut as a composer, with a little scherzo in B♭ performed under Anton Rubinstein at a recent concert of the Russian Musical Society. It had been well reviewed. But the letter is dark. In it, Modest confesses to periods of excruciating torment of a vaguely sexual nature (masturbation is mentioned outright), to terrible heavy dreams, to the "physical side of him" not keeping pace with his precocious mental development, to overstimulation and an "irritation of nerves" (an earlier letter had referred vaguely to the illnesses of "mysticism and cynicism," triggered by intensive reading). Now, gratefully, the worst was passing off. "Dear Milii, I know you love me," Modest writes. "For God's sake keep a tight rein on me during our conversations, don't let me go wild" (L, 23–24).

Throughout the following year, the letters to Balakirev reflect a strange confluence of inspired bouts of composing and incipient physical collapse. Musorgsky, ever the diligent student, was still courting favor and doing assignments – "I am putting my musical sins in order," he writes on 26 September 1860 – but he was also clearly pleased to be given a little leeway ("Thanks, Milii, for letting me off the writing of another scherzo, all the more as just now I am in no scherzoish mood . . ." [25 December 1860]). Yet some other, more stubborn tone has set in. It suggests that alongside the diligence and craving for approval there is now genuine independent musical labor, which could not find a facile outlet and took its toll on his nervous organism. "I get quite tired; composing is not easy work," he writes in mid-January 1861. "However, cold water helps."

During that January, Musorgsky made a trip to Moscow. As he had done on his first visit to Russia's ancient capital two years earlier, he sent home enthusiastic reports. Balakirev, an ardent St. Petersburg patriot, balked at this out-of-bounds show of curiosity toward what he considered to be civilization's backwater. To this reproach Modest replied: "As to my being swamped and needing to be pulled out of the swamp, I only say this – if I have talent, I will not be swamped and if my brain is stimulated, then all the more so; and if there's neither one nor the other – is it worth pulling a splinter out of the mud? Speaking plainly, there was a time when I nearly went under, not musically, but morally – and I crawled out . . . [In any case,] it is time to stop looking at me as a child, who must be led around so he won't fall down" (L, 34–35). Musorgsky had come to distinguish between the old cluster of anxieties – moral drowning (which he constantly feared) and moral support (which he continually needed) – and a new, more autonomous definition of a working friendship with Balakirev: musical support in the form of mutual respect. Warm letters between the two men continued. But the earlier dependent relation was corroded beyond repair. Balakirev did not take kindly to redefinitions of his role. In his 1881 memoir elicited by Stasov, he sounds bitter. "After 1870, I had every reason for losing ties with my circle," he wrote [that year, Balakirev suffered a nervous breakdown and withdrew from musical activity for half a decade]. "As far as who was right and who was wrong, let time be the judge."

Balakirev's mixed opinions on Modest were shared by other members of the group. "Modinka presented some sort of musical monstrosity to us – supposedly a trio to his scherzo, a huge, awkward monstrosity," Cui wrote in April 1863 to Rimsky-Korsakov, at the time absent from the capital on a naval cruise. "First some church chants of endless length and the usual Modinkian pedaling and so forth – all this is unclear, strange, awkward, by no means a trio . . ." A month later, in reference to Musorgsky's untoward enthusiasm for Serov's opera *Judith* (premiered the night before and not in favor with the Circle), Stasov exasperatedly wrote to Balakirev that "everything about him [Musorgsky] is flabby and colorless. To me he seems a perfect *idiot* . . . If he were set free to follow his own wishes and tastes, he would soon be overrun with weeds like all the rest." Several weeks later, Balakirev responded: yes, Cui definitely has talent; "R.-Korsakov is still a charming child"; "Musorgsky is practically an idiot" (L, 46–47).

The definitive weaning from Balakirev occurred only in 1867. The occasion was a curious orchestral piece Modest had long been nurturing, one of the first purely instrumental, non-texted compositions to seize and hold his imagination. He called it his "Witches" (it was later known as "St. John's Eve," "Night on Bald Mountain," and found its final home, rather incongruously, as a dream in *Sorochintsy Fair*). Balakirev didn't like it – enough, in fact, to refuse to schedule its performance without major changes. He told Modest as much. Musorgsky finally answered in September 1867. "It was not my financial worries that cast me into a depression," he wrote. "It was authorial depression – and although I'm embarrassed to confess it, it was authorial *acidification* over your evasive response to my witches. I consider, have considered, and shall continue to consider this piece a decent one, all the more so because this is the first time, after several independent trifles, that I independently took on a large-scale work ... Whether or not you agree, my friend, to put on my witches, that is, whether or not I ever hear them, I will change nothing in the general plan or in my treatment of the material, which is closely tied to the content of the picture and carried out sincerely, without pretense or imitation" (L, 99).

There is keen disappointment in this letter, to be sure. It is the desolation of a former student before a respected teacher who has failed to attend seriously to what the student knows is original work. But there is no uncertainty, anger, or pleas for support. Reading it, we should keep in mind that even Modest's early letters, in which he begs Balakirev to "keep him on a tight rein," are anxious only about aberrations of an intellectual and spiritual nature, not of a musical sort. Conventionally, 1867 marks the threshold year of Musorgsky's full maturity as a composer.

The gradual separation from Balakirev had a geographical component as well: the city of Moscow. The first, blissful trip had been in 1859. Modest had resigned his commission in July 1858, and the following summer was his first one free from military drill and camp exercises in the Guards. Colorful "mother Moscow" (which the Balakirev group, all partisans of St. Petersburg, called "Jericho," perhaps for its fortress walls but certainly for its oldness and doomedness) captivated the twenty-year-old composer. As he wrote to Balakirev at the end of June 1859, the Kremlin, the cupolas, the "smell of antiquity" in Moscow "transported him to another world." "You know," he wrote, "I had been a cosmopolite, but now there's been a sort of rebirth; everything Russian has become close to me and I would be offended if Russia were treated crudely, without ceremony; it's as if at the present time I've really begun to love her" (L, 17–18). Although in the coming years Musorgsky would toy with several vaguely "cosmopolitan" musical projects on tragic and romantic themes (incidental music to *Oedipus* and, later, an opera on Flaubert's *Salammbô*), from this point we can mark his passion for specifically Russian history.

There is more to this bedazzlement by Moscow, however, than winning over the future composer of *Boris Godunov* and *Khovanshchina* to an interest in his national past. Another enticement of the old capital was the hospitality offered by the Shilovsky family at their nearby estate of Glebovo (where, in 1877, Tchaikovsky would begin work on his *Eugene Onegin* under the same hospitable roof). The Shilovskys were great music enthusiasts and extremely wealthy. Modest stayed on that summer of 1859; he would return to spend January of 1861 and several summers thereafter. By all indications, at the Glebovo manor house he was looked after in the patriarchal manner that was so beneficial to his talent. Balakirev did not hesitate to reprimand Musorgsky for finding this Moscow "swamp," with its "limited personalities" and very rich people, exciting. Musorgsky, as we have seen, responded with some heat, insisting that he had not fallen into a swamp and that he no longer needed to be "led about."

That Balakirev so singlemindedly defended Peter's City against archaic Moscow casts his own nationalism in a curious light. Ever since St. Petersburg's founding in 1703, the two cities had been in competition. Moscow represented old histories, old buildings, old systems of rank, old or mercantile money. The city was (as Musorgsky's letter attested) inward- and backward-looking, organic, clan-based, ostentatiously religious, as opposed to St. Petersburg, a "Westernizing" city on the edge of empire and a modern bureaucratic megalopolis. It was something of an anomaly that this glittering cosmopolitan city, with its imperial court and wholly imported musical norms, was home to the first self-conscious quest for the "non-European" roots of Russian music. And in 1859, it was clearly an affront to Balakirev that his pupil Musorgsky had seen fit to augment the special "Russianizing" brand of music-making available at the Balakirev evenings in St. Petersburg with the more "limited" native intelligence of Moscow.

By 1861, then, Musorgsky's life had broadened. Freshly demobilized, the young man acquainted himself with the old capital and began to sense in himself a *Russian*, not solely a European, cultural imagination. In the process he distanced himself more emphatically from Balakirev's tutelage (although not, of course, from his musical tastes or methodology). And he reconfirmed his own aristocratic – that is, old-Russian aristocratic, manorial, leisurely – tastes, albeit supplemented with Western learning. His host and hostess at Glebovo maintained a private choir of singers and the elegant musicale was a regular event. "About the Shilovskys," Modest had written in the summer of 1859 with naive enthusiasm to poor Balakirev, who was scraping by on his income from music lessons in St. Petersburg, "their luxurious manor-house is on a hill; the English gardens are lovely . . . everything is splendid (just as it should be – rascally rich, Shilovsky is!) . . ." (L, 15–16). In this letter we hear Borodin's elegant "toy officer" speaking, wholly comfortable in the highest society. However realistically Musorgsky would come to portray beggars, holy fools, hungry orphans, and shrewish wives in his songs and historical operas, and however much his basic decency forbade him to complain of his own altered personal circumstances, such luxury would remain his natural home.

Yet it was the final year of its kind. The Emancipation legislation went into effect two months after Modest took leave of the Shilovskys, with whom he had spent a month of the holiday season in January 1861. Estate owners in the Shilovskys' bracket were too rich to be undone by the Reform. More typical of the marginal untitled nobility was the Musorgskys' fate. During the next two years, income from their lands steadily worsened. As a result, in 1863 the younger son was obliged to take up a "bureaucratic career."

What had the family resources been? On the eve of the Emancipation, the Musorgsky family owned 10,000 *desiatines* of land, or roughly 27,000 acres.[4] This property included eighteen villages, with a population of 193 "audited souls" (adult male serfs on record since the last census). Adding women and children, the total was upwards of four hundred peasants. Serf villages across Russia discharged their obligations to their masters through a variety of payment schedules: labor-days, deliveries in kind, and cash. As part of the 1861 legislation, serfs were to be freed with land. But because property worked by peasants belonged in part to the commune and in part to the landlords (and because peasants and their masters often had very different notions of ownership rights), there was no natural coincidence of interests between the two classes. It took hard bargaining on particulars to arrive at a just settlement.

The Musorgskys' situation was more complicated than their neighbors'. The eighteen villages were well aware that the matriarch Yulia Ivanovna was widowed and of gentle hospitable disposition, that Karevo had long been a haven for the indigent and hangers-on, and that the two sons were now city dwellers, out of touch with peasant life. It was also no secret that the sons' grandmother had been a peasant woman herself, although "gentrified"; dozens of "relatives" were still alive in the villages. They would press for the most profitable bargain possible. The unpleasant task of negotiating fell to the firstborn Filaret. Given the pressure, and assuming a certain degree of self-interest and foul play on all sides, Filaret was, it appears, fair – but he was harsh. Modest, his mother's son, was in all ways softer.

All evidence suggests that Modest was grateful to his brother for taking over primary responsibility in this matter of transferring property, for he had few economic instincts himself. When his finances changed, he adjusted to reality by taking a menial job and working at it in an undistinguished fashion. Genuine aristocrats are not demeaned by activity they agree to do. And by temperament, it seems, Modest was just that sort of old-regime, pre-Emancipation aristocrat (along the lines of Count Ilya Rostov in Tolstoy's *War and Peace*): kind, generous, physically lazy, impractical, unwilling to keep careful accounts and thus easily and irreversibly in debt. What he could not do was bully, cheat, drive a hard bargain, or stand up for his rights. Surely this is what his more practical brother Filaret, scarred after years of negotiations with recalcitrant former serfs and scoundrelly stewards, meant when he wrote in his memoir – and he had a point – that his younger sibling "considered the Russian peasant a real human being (in this he was sadly mistaken). As a result of this attitude, he suffered material losses and hardship."

In letters to friends from these years, Modest speaks frankly of his financial situation and state of mind. His helplessness, sense of humor, and inbred dignity are all in clear view. As he wrote to César Cui in June 1863 from Toropets (one of the family's villages): the overseer had played a dirty trick with the estate, and if it weren't for his mother who needed him, he would not be there at all. The local landlords were all boors, crybabies, brawlers, "every day they pester you tearfully with their lost rights, their total ruin . . . such howlings, moanings, scandal!" There were some decent young fellows who actually negotiated with the peasants – but they were never to be seen, Musorgsky notes, for they were always on the road. "So I, for my sins, revolve in this *latrine-like* atmosphere. A latrine atmosphere rarely touches the finer instincts; one thinks only how not to make a stink or else how not to suffocate (how can one even think of music here!)" (L, 55–56).

This letter to Cui speaks volumes. Musorgsky, finding himself in crude or unpleasant circumstances, does not join the chorus of complainers but rather distances himself, tries not to exacerbate the situation, stylizes it, draws a comic (or tragicomic) picture of it. Such was his means of coping. All his life, Musorgsky was a stupendous illustrator. It was often the experience of incommensurable loss that stimulated his visual, and from there his dramatic and then musical imagination. The purest achievement in this realm is probably *Pictures from an Exhibition*, commemorating a dear, dead friend; the greatest operatic expression of such comprehensive and irretrievable loss is *Khovanshchina*, which chronicles the death of an entire culture. When unexpectedly deprived of support that was necessary to him, Musorgsky was not the sort who sought out help, re-educated himself, or cast about for the best pragmatic solution. For a time, he might break down. Then he would rally and create a world – a dramatized musical world – that lived on its own.

Modest Petrovich remained poorly equipped to deal with new post-Emancipation realities. Expertise in that area took time and a special sort of intelligence. But he was no "crybaby and brawler." To Balakirev that same month he announced wryly that he could not live on the income of his estates and must "enter into a career of service, to feed and pamper my delicate body" (L, 54). In December 1863, six months after the letter to Cui about the "*latrine-like* atmosphere" of Toropets, Musorgsky took a position in the imperial bureaucracy. Since he had retired from the Guards so young, his entrance rank was very low. For a month and a half he worked in the Central Engineering Authority at the level of collegiate secretary; at the end of January 1864, he was appointed assistant chief of the barracks division of the Authority. (The salary for this sort of work was a pittance, and there was no way he could have supported himself on it alone. Even during his second stint of service – this time with the Forestry Department in the Ministry of State Domains, in the late 1860s – and already with some seniority and experience, Musorgsky's annual income was 450 rubles, about $350.) In December 1866, Musorgsky was promoted to assistant head clerk, with the rank of titular counselor; this show of approval was a hopeful sign. But in April 1867 he was dismissed from his post in a routine downsizing of the department. He was allowed to remain in service but would collect no wages.[5]

How demeaning and invasive was this clerical work? Sometime during the summer of 1867 Balakirev (himself temporarily in funds because of his expanding official musical activities), together with other well-meaning friends, made an offer of help to Musorgsky. In September, Modest wrote a tactful response. He was grateful, but, as he assured Balakirev,

> in the present situation, I regard myself as *not justified* in alarming my friends and deceiving them; their disposition toward me is too valuable. My means have shrunk. This is true; but not so far as to deprive me of any possibility of an autonomous existence. Being accustomed to material plenty and even in part to luxury, I am, in the present circumstances, not completely calm about the future and it is hardly surprising that I made a wry face . . . [but] I implore you to be calm on my account and reassure all those dear to me. Their fear for me weighs unbearably heavy, and my situation does not merit it. It is all the heavier because I am more afraid of deceit than I am of anything else. . . . All who sincerely love me will be happier to see me existing independently, rather than flashing across the sky like some meteor . . . calm my friends and yourself, this you *must* do, because I adjure you out of fear of deception, that most foul of all evils. (L, 98)

This 1867 letter to Balakirev is the same one in which Musorgsky remarks on his "authorial acidification" over the poor reception given his witches – a composition he did not intend to alter, even in the face of his mentor's disapproval. Modest's stance in his epistolary relationship with Balakirev can thus be seen to have shifted across a wide front. He no longer courted favor or apologized for his work. He did not wish his friends to pry too closely into his financial situation. Most importantly, deceit or deception – *obman* – was singled out as the worst of human sins.

The early 1860s mark the beginning of Musorgsky's search for a surrogate family. His own agreeable domestic arrangements were breaking up. Having salvaged a portion of the estate, Filaret married in 1862, while Yulia Ivanovna, unable to maintain the expense of the townhouse, moved back to Karevo in 1863. Modest took up his clerk-ship in the Engineering Authority, boarding for a while with his married brother in St. Petersburg. But that set-up must have felt tem-porary. For the first time in his life, Modest found himself alone – and during the very period when he was growing restless under Balakirev's tutelage. His initial solution was the "Loginov Commune" (so named after the three brothers who constituted half of its mem-bership), a collective living arrangement with five other young men in the gloomy Stenbok-Fermor house overlooking the Catherine Canal in a noisy, run-down St. Petersburg neighborhood. It was to last somewhat over two years. In his 1881 biographical sketch, Stasov laconically introduces this phase in the composer's life:

> In the fall of 1863, upon his return from the countryside, [Musorgsky] settled, together with several young comrades, in a shared apartment which they jokingly called a "commune." Perhaps it was in imitation of the theory of communal living preached at that time in [Chernyshevsky's] famous novel *What is To Be Done?*. Each of the comrades had his separate room, where no other person was allowed to enter without special permission granted each time; there was also a large common room where they would all gather in the evening, when free from their official duties, to read, listen to readings, converse, argue, simply talk – or to listen to Musorgsky playing the piano, singing romances and excerpts from operas. There must have been no small number of such little comradely communities in St. Petersburg at the time, and perhaps, in the rest of Russia as well.[6]

In all likelihood, the six young men (almost nothing is known of them beyond their names) were not merely joking when they called their housing arrangement a "commune." During the 1860s, such innovative experiments in everyday living were taken very seriously by progressive Russian intellectuals. Musorgsky eagerly counted himself among their number; indeed, he was to complain throughout his life that musicians, regretfully, were not expected to have ideas. (When, in the summer of 1870, his realistic-satirical song "The Seminarist" was prohibited by ecclesiastical censorship, Musorgsky seemed almost pleased; for as he wrote to Stasov, "this ban shows that from being 'nightingales, leafy forests and lovers singing in the moonlight,' musicians have become members of human societies" [L, 152].) Although he probably made too light of this living arrangement, Stasov was otherwise correct to mention in connection with it Chernyshevsky's progressive-utopian novel *What is To Be Done?*, a scandalous bestseller upon its publication in 1863. The details that Stasov mentions – separate professions but shared intellectual life, strict contracts among the members concerning privacy – strongly suggest that this novel, and probably other teachings by its author as well, were indeed an inspiration for the Loginov commune.

What were these ideas that proved so attractive to Musorgsky? Unfortunately the composer – a voracious reader but by the end of his life, a homeless one – left no library. We may fairly assume, however, that he was familiar with the aesthetics of Nikolai Chernyshevsky (1828–89), the journalist, novelist, and lay philosopher whose radical opinions on "realism in art" were widely discussed in the 1850s–60s and probably influenced, in indirect fashion, Musorgsky's musical practice. But it is Chernyshevsky's social and philosophical views that have relevance to the experiment of the commune and Musorgsky's search for stable family.[7] During his adolescence, Modest had read widely in German idealist and Romantic philosophy. In his early confessional letters to Balakirev, he had blamed "mysticism" and "idealism" for his recurring nervous collapse. To this impressionable young man, ideas were almost morbidly important.

And the cornerstone of Chernyshevsky's system, enunciated most clearly in his 1860 essay "The Anthropological Principle in Philosophy," was its frontal attack against the entire German idealist philosophical tradition. That tradition, so nourishing to European Romanticism and later to Symbolism, taught the value of transcendence over "unreal" or "fallen" matter and endorsed a dual vision of the human being as mortal body and immortal soul. In opposition to this doctrine, Chernyshevsky insisted that human beings had a single unified nature in the sublunary world. Thus products of human nature – such as art – should strive for "non-idealistic" understandings of the sublime, the tragic, the beautiful, the real. But human production is not just a heap of static products. A non-idealistic ethos also mandates that we experience life itself as a sort of dynamic aesthetic process. Mutual respect, domestic stability, productive work, a steady and reliable source of energy in our lives, a high degree of good sense brought to every task, and most of all happiness in love: these were the criteria for true humanness. The progressive heroes and heroines of *What is To Be Done?* (the so-called "New People") attempt to live their lives – somewhat idyllically, and definitely under a lucky star – in just this spirit.

Chernyshevsky's novel is a strange St. Petersburg tale. Although cast in the drab, cold, slum-ridden capital, its radiant personalities have nothing in common with the criminals, madmen, self-appointed martyrs and ascetics that populate the urban narratives of Gogol and Dostoevsky (or for that matter, of Dickens and Balzac). Its characters apply a utilitarian standard to their lives – and find this easy and pleasant to do. The novel's heroine Vera Pavlovna, although wholly inexperienced, organizes a seamstresses' cooperative and their work turns a profit. Disagreements (even over triangular affairs of the heart) are settled amicably. The love that is valued in the novel is not of the frenzied Romantic Tristan-and-Isolde sort, with mutual fidelity dependent upon mutual suicide, but cheerful, sustained, contented, growing richer with time. As the narrator instructs Vera Pavlovna (herself the beneficiary of several devoted "husbands"), by its very nature love is happy and carefree. As have realists before and since, Chernyshevsky wished to demystify erotic love. Its demands would yield to the proper hygiene. The needs of matter and of spirit did not require sacrificing one to the other. This doctrine, aristocratic in essence and a thinking man's utopia, must have seemed to the hypersensitive Musorgsky the clarion call of good health.

How does one set up such a life? Chernyshevsky was not a cold rationalist, nor was he a mystic or a dreamer. Like Musorgsky, he was interested in being (for want of a better word) an accurate anthropologist. Intensely interested in womens' rights, and sharing the general Russian cultural bias against men (considered superfluous, trivial, theoretical) in favor of women (presumed to be intuitive, indispensable, practical, kind), Chernyshevsky attributed much importance to daily ritual and domestic architectural layouts. Such rituals, he felt, always affect women's lives intimately: the right to close a door, to maintain a private life, to not be interrupted without warning or reason. Only by attending to these everyday details could genuine equality – and thus community – be sustained. Sexuality is certainly present in his fictional plots and physical love between men and women is acknowledged as a pleasure, but there was little of the neurotic, possessive, or self-destructive in sexual expression. In Chernyshevsky's novel, erotic love creates exciting topics of discussion, but no unsolvable problems. Ideas in circulation, one suspects, are the real muse.

How might the Loginov commune be connected with this bestselling novel and its controversial author? Unlike the collective arrangements in the novel, it contained no women. It also contained no other musicians. Musorgsky found there the pattern that defined the maternal homestead as well: someone always "home," a maximum of body warmth, shared housekeeping rituals – but minimal creative interference. He could perform music (although most likely not his own) without submitting it for approval. The intellectual level was high. Physical intimacy was not a threat and did not arouse expectations that could not be satisfied; thus deception and deceit were less likely. Stasov, with his customary vague hyperbole, wrote in 1881 that "the three years [two is meant] that the young men spent under this new arrangement were, according to their own accounts, among the best years of their lives. And for Musorgsky especially."[8]

Stasov was partially correct. But those years could hardly have been idyllic. The neighborhood was grimy, the bureaucratic work tedious;

moreover, Musorgsky's beloved mother died in 1865, triggering a terrible, prolonged bout of drinking in her younger son. Filaret, in his memoir, refers frankly to this episode as the "onset of a terrible disease (*delirium tremens*)" (MR, 27). "In the fall of 1865," he writes, "my wife forced him [Modest] to leave the commune and brought him home to us, at first against his will." One can only imagine what a ghastly reduction and redefinition of family love this move must have signified for so proud and pampered a child. For the years preceding the commune period, 1861–63, had been a time of intense technical study by the autodidact Musorgsky. As he put it later, he had been "acquiring useful knowledge" and "putting his brains in order," creating exercises, transcriptions, and numerous study pieces, including a piano four-hands arrangement of most of Beethoven's String Quartet, Op. 130 (L, 41). In the commune, he began to compose in earnest.

These compositions tended to be in the grand operatic style, ambitious and then abandoned. In October 1863, influenced by Alexander Serov's tremendously successful epic opera *Judith* premiered earlier that year, Musorgsky began work on a libretto for an opera based on Flaubert's *Salammbô*. (The commune had just finished a collective reading of that novel.) Musorgsky produced large segments of text and music simultaneously in 1863 and 1864, much of it later recycled in *Boris Godunov*; ultimately, however, only three full scenes were sketched, in what the composer called "piano draft." It is of some interest to consider which scenes Musorgsky, with his vivid dramatic imagination, chose to set from Flaubert's melodramatic and exotic love story.

The novel's plot is an absolute cliché. The beautiful daughter (Salammbô) of a powerful Oriental tyrant (Hamilcar) falls in love with the rebel challenger to the Carthaginian throne (Mâtho), former slave and now commander-in-chief of the Libyans. The conventional erotic tension of this plot – one might even say, its naturally operatic parts – interested the composer not at all. The scenes he finished (scene 2 of Act 2, scene 1 of Act 3, scene 1 of Act 4) deal with criminal action

(Mâtho stealing the sacred veil from the Temple of Tanit), choral-sacrificial mass spectacle (children being fed alive to the flames as a propitiatory offering, to the wailing of women), or solitary lamentation (Mâtho in the dungeon in chains, awaiting his death sentence). The one episode that routinely characterizes an "exotic southern" opera of this imperial sort – think of Borodin's *Prince Igor* and its sensuous Polovtsian core – is noticeably absent: the love and seduction duet, in this case Salammbô offering her virginity to Mâtho in order to retrieve the sacred veil and save Carthage. Musorgsky was simply not inspired by Eros as he was by Thanatos, by mass uprisings, and by crime. Appropriately, while working on the opera he changed its title to *Liviets*, "The Libyan."

And so we arrive at the vexed biographical – emotional and physiological – question of Musorgsky and erotic love. There has been much speculation, although very little data. Some of it was local lore: for example, the story circulating among Karevo residents that Modest as a teenager had been in love with a female cousin who (conveniently) died and was interred with a packet of letters from Modest in her coffin; ever after he remained faithful to her memory. Some stories seem constructed defensively by family members (most probably the prim Filaret) to ward off rumors: for example, the tale, repeated by Filaret's granddaughter Tatiana Georgievna at age eighty-eight to her interviewer Novikov in 1984, that there was "love for a certain woman to whom he made a proposal, but she refused him because she was a great deal older; but she watched over him until her death and preserved friendly relations; and 'that's why he never married.' This view was passed down in the family from generation to generation."9 Delirious but inconclusive research has been devoted to identifying the dedicatees of Musorgsky's few (and relatively feeble) lyrical love songs, especially the woman most often so honored, Nadezhda Opochinina. Mme. Shilovskaya, amateur singer and wealthy, gracious hostess of Glebovo, received one such song from Musorgsky, set to a suggestive text ("What mean the words of love?") – but by all indications this was a *pièce d'occasion*, given in gratitude for hospitality extended.[10] Musorgsky was not a wealthy man. He thanked his benefactors, male as well as female, with the only capital he could generate: his songs, his manuscripts, his dramatic scenes.

Then there is more concrete biographical evidence. Musorgsky hints in his early letters to Balakirev of nervous disorders stemming from an "insufficient development of his physical side," which he was treating with gymnastics and cold bathing. In the January 1861 letter to Balakirev from Moscow, in which he speaks of being pulled out of a swamp and notes how he almost "went under, not musically but morally," Musorgsky added (and the phrase sounds rather crude in Russian) "if you must know, there was a woman involved."[11] But references to women as women are extremely rare in his personal writings. Even in an era when intense male bonding was the norm and perceived as wholly compatible with heterosexual appetite, Musorgsky's emotional dependence on men was probably extreme, and he did not outgrow it. The loss of two housemates, Rimsky-Korsakov in 1872 and Golenishchev-Kutuzov in 1875, both to marriage, was a terrible blow to him; although he did make amends to the men and their wives (he was best man at their weddings), he clearly felt abandoned – and perhaps betrayed. Then there is a lurid anecdote, recorded by Liudmila Shestakova (Glinka's sister and patroness to the Balakirev circle) to the effect that Musorgsky's "disinclination for marriage reached the point of absurdity; more than once, he seriously assured me that if I were to read in the papers the news that he had shot or hanged himself, it meant that he had gotten married the day before" (MR, 54).

Although not a handsome man, Musorgsky – with his delicacy, wit, and (for those with ears to hear) extraordinary talent – appealed to women. One who was especially attracted was the elder of the two Purgold sisters, Aleksandra. While still in their teens, these two independently minded, musically gifted sisters (they lived in a family of seven brothers, one floor above Dargomyzhsky's apartment) became indispensable to the Balakirev evenings and a mainstay of the group's informal concertizing in St. Petersburg. The younger Purgold sister,

8 The Purgold sisters: (left) Aleksandra Nikolaevna, later Mme. Molas (1845–1929);
(right) Nadezhda Nikolaevna, later Mme. Rimsky-Korsakov (1848–1919)

Nadezhda, was a composer and pianist; Musorgsky's epithet for her was "our dear little orchestra." In 1872 she became the wife of Rimsky-Korsakov. The elder sister Aleksandra, an amateur singer of unusual flexibility who proved herself a superb performer of Musorgsky's realistic songs, promptly married Nikolai Molas that same year.

Aleksandra Purgold had long been waiting on Musorgsky. In a diary entry for August 1870, Nadezhda, at the time twenty-two, remarked of her twenty-six-year-old sister:

> it is time for her to *have a husband*. However, she sees only coldness in the man [Musorgsky] who might inspire passion in her if only he would show a little more interest in her . . . Some people think he isn't very intelligent, but I don't agree. He has his own kind of brain, original and very witty. True, he sometimes misuses this wit . . . But all the same, I can't understand his relation to Sasha [Aleksandra]. It seems to me that she interests him, but whether he is able to be attracted to her, to fall in love with her, that I don't know. He is an egotist, a terrific egotist! (L, 154–55).

We find here all the usual charges leveled against non-heterosexuals: biting wit, inexplicable distance, bantering friendship with women who would prefer to arouse other feelings, accusations of cruelty and egotism.

Finally there is the corpus of Musorgsky's music itself. There are no love songs above the level of mediocrity. In his *Salammbô* project, conventional love scenes did not appeal. Nor did they appeal in *Boris Godunov*, conceived four years later and initially rejected for performance by the Imperial Opera Commission because it lacked love interest and a prima donna role (even in the Polish act added to the revised opera, "love scenes" are more a matter of two people aping desire for political ends). And the Eros in *Khovanshchina*, as we shall see in chapter 4, is of a peculiar sort. Kidnapping and rape there is, as well as competition between father and son for the same maiden and some incidental lust for dancing slaves. But for the "romantic leads" there are no true love duets at all. Love is the province of soothsaying; the lyric tenor calls his mistress a witch and tries to stab her on stage; eventually, Eros transforms itself into a quest for salvation through mass suicide. Superficial resemblances here to the mutual commitment we find in the real love-and-death operas – such as Wagner's *Tristan and Isolde*, premiered in 1865 – are wholly illusory. In "Serenade," probably the sexiest of the four *Songs and Dances of Death* composed in the mid-1870s, Death visits a dying girl and courts her in words far more seductive than any a living suitor could offer. We can fairly conclude that a reciprocated erotic feeling on the part of a living woman did not inspire Musorgsky's muse.

We are unlikely to learn anything more about Musorgsky's sexual orientation. He had no known partners. He felt loneliness intensely. He was grateful to older women and gallant with younger ones, but made no secret of his extreme "disinclination for marriage." In this as in so much else, the composer more resembles the evasive, masked Gogol than he does the urbane Tchaikovsky (for whom homosexuality was an open secret and homoerotic behavior a traceable part of the biography). Before we leave this topic and chapter, however, one more hypothesis might be offered. Its starting point is in an early letter to Balakirev; the reference is to another then-contemporary novel.

In a letter dated 19 October 1859, the twenty-year-old Modest, having just survived a bout with "mysticism," thanks Milii for his friendship during that ordeal and then makes the following comment: "I finished *Oblomov* today and have already argued with *maman* about love, with Kitusha supporting me. In the fourth part, love is absolutely explained – love of an Oblomov sort, to be sure, but love all the same. Only you're not right, Milii, in one thing: no woman, no matter what sort, could fall in love with Oblomov, only an Agafya Matveyevna could."[12] This passing reference is worth pursuing, for clearly the novel had been a topic of discussion between the three young men – in keeping, we might add, with the time-honored Russian habit of analyzing the self in terms of novelistic prototypes.

What and who is Oblomov, and who is Agafya Matveyevna? Might this comment prompt us to an insight into Musorgsky, his mother, and the means by which the young Modest believed love could be "absolutely explained"?

Ivan Goncharov finished his novel *Oblomov* in 1858. It became an instant bestseller, just as Chernyshevsky's *What Is To Be Done?* would five years later – and as with that later novel, the "thinking intelligentsia" in Russia seized on the chance to measure itself against a fictional model. The hero, Ilya Oblomov, is an intelligent, sensitive, sheltered nobleman, raised by doting parents in an idyllic rural spot. When the novel opens, he is already on his own in St. Petersburg. Most of his time is spent lying down. In fact, for fully half of Part One, he avoids getting up from his couch altogether. Visitors come and go, bad news is received from the rascally bailiff of his estates, but he simply avoids dealing with it and dozes off. His name soon became synonymous with Russian sloth. "Oblomovshchina" [Oblomov-itis], a word built off the same logic and suffix as "Khovanshchina," entered the Russian language in the 1860s as a collective noun for all the sins and vices connected with the Oblomov-type personality.

Oblomov's best friend, Andrei Stolz, is an efficient Russified German who spends a great deal of energy trying to prod Ilya into activity. In one of those odd quirks of the heart, Oblomov does, for several chapters, come to active life. Almost against his will, he falls in love with the vivacious, musically gifted Olga Ilyinskaya, who returns his love and is proud at having aroused it. They decide to marry. But in a plot reminiscent of Gogol's play *Marriage*, the whole thing somehow dwindles out: Oblomov cannot get out of the lease for his lodgings, he has no idea of the income from his estate, his bailiff won't answer his letters so he cannot set a date for the wedding (or even announce the betrothal). Most tellingly, he is terrified when he realizes that Olga expects from him a sustained passionate response. "All that is very well in poetry or on the stage," he remarks to himself early in the novel, ruminating about love. But in real life, passion "is like gunpowder: an explosion – and afterwards, deafness and blindness." For

Oblomov, perfect love (and he often dreams of that image) is unchangeably calm, sympathetic, and thoughtful.

Olga eventually marries Stolz. With the collapse of his own wedding plans, Oblomov falls seriously ill; he begins to recover only through the ministrations of his landlady, a simple, hardworking civil servant's widow, one Agafya Matveyevna. She devotes herself to his well-being, beggaring herself and her children to provide him with asparagus and sturgeon. Stolz rescues Oblomov's estate – but several years later, he is appalled to discover that the highborn Oblomov has fathered a son with this undistinguished commoner. Oblomov himself is back dozing on the couch; when he dies of heart failure, Stolz snatches up the son and raises him together with his own energetic brood. In Part Four of the novel, Olga is already Stolz's wife. She comes to understand that her former love for Oblomov – however sincerely felt at the time – was self-deception. Given this resolution, what might the young Modest Petrovich have meant when he remarked in his letter to Balakirev that by the end of Goncharov's novel "love had received its perfect explanation," and that "no woman, but only an Agafya Matveyevna" could commit herself to the demands of an Oblomov-style love?

Musorgsky, of course, was no Oblomov. Although he often chided himself for his "Russian laziness" and apathetic metabolism, he had no lack of creative energy. Raised by doting and overprotective parents, "doughily" given to dreaming and reading throughout his life, Musorgsky was, nevertheless, ambitious in his own way. In Goncharov's great and subtle novel, however, he must have sensed a dynamic – or better, perhaps, an economy – of means and ends. "Oblomov-style love" is designed to protect a creative gift from the onrush of the world. It comes to the aid of those who are helpless in practical matters, and it requires not sexual passion (which is disruptive, invasive, and always generates new obligations) but steadfast provisioning. Agafya Matveyevna is a woman, of course, and bears Oblomov's child; but nothing much is made of that event in the novel. It is an afterthought, a byproduct of more primary services: Agafya is most attractive to Oblomov when she is briskly chopping vegetables in the kitchen, her white elbows flashing. She becomes a mother without, as it were, obliging Oblomov to become a lover.

Reading Part Four, the young Modest Musorgsky was convinced that no woman – that is, no Olga Ilyinskaya with normal female expectations – could love a man with Oblomov-like needs. No wonder that his mother, who catered to those needs so invisibly, argued with him about it. It was her desire that both her sons follow their father's example into an active, independent life. The elder Filaret worried her less. But at twenty, this favored second son was far from fully formed. He had already been writing to Balakirev for two years about recurring nervous attacks, physical sluggishness, underdevelopment, "excruciating sufferings" beyond what ordinary adolescence should have extracted. Striking out on his own would not be easy. Fortunately, the status of progenitor or "head of household" was not the only marker of full maturity in pre-reform Russia. Rural society, and certainly the cluttered Karevo homestead of Modinka's childhood, never knew the nuclear family. Russian gentry life was inclusive and tolerant; the genius, the misfit, the odd bachelor son or daughter could always find a protective corner and abundant love.

If there must be labels for such delicate matters in a biography, then, I suggest that Musorgsky's life be spared the standard rubrics: homophilic, heterosexual, and their numerous "repressed" variants. That axis is not the only one along which energy can flow – or be obstructed. Musorgsky was raised with his mother's standards: tact, an obligation to provide an atmosphere of cheerful calm, gentleness in the face of others' anger, the ability to retreat and fall silent when attacked. All this bespeaks a person who knows the cost of human interaction and desires most of all not to feed expectations that cannot be satisfied, such that would involve him in deceit or deception, "that most foul of evils." It appears that Musorgsky craved a life where material provisioning came first and effortlessly (the Shilovsky estate where "everything is splendid, just as it should be," or the world of Agafya Matveyevna). Under such conditions he could begin to work.

Passion, that "torch set to gunpowder," was relegated to those safer realms where Oblomov had exiled it: in poetry and on the stage. In 1865, Musorgsky was twenty-six. It was impossible to reclaim his prior favorite-son position in his own safe, once nurturing family. He hadn't a notion how to set up a family himself. The passion was ready to go on stage.

3 Conservatories, "circles," and Musorgsky at the far musical edge

In January 1861, in the St. Petersburg journal *The Age* [*Vek*], the great piano virtuoso Anton Rubinstein published a bombshell article entitled "The State of Music in Russia."[1] Its appearance would have been unthinkable several years earlier. Under Tsar Nicholas I (1825–55), the rights of Russian subjects did not include the right to address the public on current events directly and in writing, and certainly not in a disputatious tone. But after Russia's humiliating defeat in the Crimean War and the ascension of Alexander II (1855–81), the government began to tolerate – and then actively to encourage – a growing tidal wave of national self-examination. Although short-lived, it was a heady and optimistic time. Censorship was loosened; a shared civic language and "polemical journal culture" developed almost overnight. Angers long pent up became articulate. If Slavophiles had looked backward to the past for Russia's salvation and Westernizers forward to her modernization, then during this brief period of glasnost Russians were at last legally permitted to look at Russia's *present* and address its concrete ills. The reform years, 1859–64, touched all aspects of economic, social, and cultural life.

Within that half-decade wedge, the institutional life of music in Russia was born. On the "official" side, the major players were Anton Rubinstein's Russian Musical Society, founded with royal patronage in 1859, and its formal successor, the St. Petersburg Conservatory, which opened (also under Rubinstein) in September 1862. On the

"unofficial" side were the Balakirev Circle of musicians – and its
offspring in the realm of pedagogy, also launched in 1862, the "Free
Music School." (The "Free" of the title is neither metaphysical nor
political but simply economic: *besplatnaya*, "free of charge.")
Although they shared some of the same patrons, personnel, and cur-
riculum, from the start their missions were different. Such was the
rhetoric surrounding their setting-up, however, that bitter rivalry
between the two organizations was inevitable, at least in the press.
Stasov and Cui, public personalities par excellence, entered the fray.

Musorgsky was not a public orator. His language was too crooked
and idiosyncratic, his response to things (even in those outspoken
times) too unmonitored. In April 1862, from the village of Volok, he
wrote to Milii Balakirev about the new musical options in St.
Petersburg:

> I *exult* in your successful concerts and I *wish health* to the newborn
> school! . . . In Peter, with only an insignificant distance between
> them, two schools have been formed, absolute contrasts in
> character. One is *Professoria*; the other, a free association of *kindred*
> spirits in art. In one, Zaremba and Tupinstein, in their professorial,
> anti-musical togas, *stuff* the heads of their students with various
> abominations and infect them in advance. The poor pupils see before
> them not *human beings* but two fixed pillars to which are nailed some
> idiotic scrawls said to contain the *laws of music*. But Tupinstein is *tup*
> [dull] – thus he scrupulously does his duty: *to be maliciously dull*. (L,
> 43–44)

The letter continues in this bantering, crude fashion, replete with
unprintable obscenities about the Grand Duchess Elena Pavlovna,
widowed sister-in-law of the late Emperor, a German by birth and
patroness of the Conservatory, and resonant as well with that insiderly
anti-Semitism ("Tupinstein"/Rubinstein) widespread among the
Russian aristocracy. A document like this should not be over-read; it is
a private letter, not a policy statement for a public forum, and its contents are conditioned by what the letter-writer knew its recipient
wanted to hear. Still, Musorgsky's intemperate reaction to the

Conservatory suggests that something deep was at stake for him in this rivalry. What was it? How did it affect his efforts between 1862 and 1868 to arrive at a dramatically valid "musical realism," and how did it conduce to his gradual alienation from members of the Balakirev Circle?

By 1861, Musorgsky had composed only a handful of works: one song in the folk style, a drinking song, several romances, three unfinished piano sonatas, two scherzos for piano. Most of these were still exercises for Balakirev. But Musorgsky's opinions about musical composition were stubbornly set. In January of that year, he wrote from Moscow an agitated letter to Balakirev in the northern capital.

> A propos, on the train I read a new magazine, *Vek*, with an article by A. Rubinstein. He says that in Russia there are not and never have been musician-artists, but there have been and are *musician-amateurs*; he bases this conclusion on the fact that the genuine artist works *for glory and money*, and not for anything else, and then he clinches the argument by saying that it is impossible to call anyone an artist and proclaim him a talent who has written less than three or four good things during his lifetime. What *prerogatives* does Rubinstein have for such limited definitions – *glory and money*, and *quantity rather than quality*? *O Océan! O Puddle.* (L, 31; the aquatic references are to Rubinstein's Second Symphony in C major, Op. 42, known as the "Ocean Symphony")

Although Musorgsky's paraphrase of his opponent's position is wholly unjust, it does provide some valuable insight into his own psychology. Let us lay out the debate, and then consider why the twenty-two-year-old Musorgsky might have felt so pinched and threatened by the opposing side.

Anton Rubinstein (1829–94) had returned to his native Russia in 1848 after musical training in Berlin and a precocious European career as piano child prodigy.[2] Among the many things that struck him as antediluvian upon his return was the low (technically, the non-existent) status of Russian musicians. Sculptors, painters, and actors had achieved the rank of "free artist" under Empress Catherine II,

9 Anton Rubinstein (1829–1894), piano virtuoso and founder of the
   St. Petersburg Conservatory

which turned them, in effect, into legal citizens: those three categories of artist were exempted from the poll tax and military service and
awarded the right to move freely about the Empire without permis-
sion. No such status had been granted to musicians. (Rubinstein himself was mortified that all his musical accomplishments could not
earn him an appellation on his passport more accurate than "son of a
merchant of the second guild.") In 1852, Rubinstein was appointed
personal accompanist to the court of the Grand Duchess Elena
Pavlovna. But his concern for the state of music in Russia was such
that he hungered for more than individual, virtuosic success.

In 1859, with the backing of the Grand Duchess, Rubinstein
founded the Russian Musical Society. It sponsored a series of symphonic concerts as well as a network of classes in the fundamentals of
music theory and in voice, piano, violin, and cello. These lessons,
open to Russians at no cost or at only nominal fee, were taught by outstanding musicians – understandably, most of them foreigners or
Russians who had trained abroad. Many donated their services gratis.
The Society was a huge step toward increasing musical literacy in St.
Petersburg. But it did not resolve the question of professionalism in
music, nor did it alter the fact that Russian musicians could not regis-
ter officially in their craft. For this, an accredited conservatory was
necessary.

The concept of such a school was relatively new, even in Western
Europe. As the reform spirit gained momentum, Rubinstein put his
considerable prestige behind his 1861 article in *The Age*. An official
diploma would grant its graduates the civic status of musician, per-
mitting them to earn their living in Russia as music teachers to the
population at large (music lessons would then not be denied to those
Russians without command of foreign languages). It would encourage full-time devotion to musical art, at that time perceived largely as a
social pastime or gentleman's leisurely pursuit. And lastly, a conservatory would foster a professional guild mentality. This latter gain was
especially precious, Rubinstein believed, because the responsible
practice of any art must protect itself from two extremes. At one pole,

there was the danger of art at the mercy of the mob, art as the victim of popular taste or shifting fashion. At the other was the equal (and for the creative musician, perhaps even greater) danger inherent in "the immunity of the amateur."

Amateurs, Rubinstein argued, partake of art for their personal pleasure and thus avoid what causes them discomfort. They surround themselves with like-minded enthusiasts and feel no need to submit to the judgment of critics; in fact, they can with impunity "regard the ill-intentioned critic with scorn." Even among themselves, there is no bottom line for basic skills and no special respect for shared standards. The acid test, Rubinstein observes, is the ensemble: get yourself invited to a "home which considers itself musical" and you will see that everyone can play some piece or sing some aria, "but try to get them to play or sing something together – a trio or quartet – and you will find that it is impossible." The amateur composer will likewise cobble together some little song, get it published, become a "musical celebrity" in his own town, "will endlessly compose romances without noticing that they are all repetitions of the same melody, will not want to grasp the rules of harmony and composition, will start to contend that only melody has value in music, and that everything else is German pedantry; and he will end up composing an opera." Rubinstein admits that some amateurs do study music theory. "But here too they do not behave like true artists," he added. "They value not the rules but the exceptions; and once having assimilated these exceptions, they never give them up." "People will argue that great geniuses have rarely come out of conservatoires," he concludes. "I agree; but who can deny that good musicians come out of them, and that is precisely what is essential in our enormous country."[3] Genius will develop regardless of schools; teachers and professionals will not.

One month later, in the journal The Northern Bee, Stasov answered Rubinstein's policy statement with a windy screed of his own.[4] "Mr. Rubinstein is a foreigner," Stasov began. Thus "he understands neither Russian national character nor Russian historical develop-

10   Vladimir Stasov (portrait by Ilya Repin, 1873)

ment." This was as incorrect as it was nastily racist: Rubinstein was
born in the Russian Empire, baptized in the Orthodox Church. On
two counts, however, both relevant to Musorgsky, Stasov's rebuttal
cannot be dismissed. Our dilettantes are no more harmful than amateurs in other countries, Stasov observes. But given Russia's high

level of cultural centralization, her bureaucratic rigidity, the passion of her subjects for favors dispensed by the state, and the overall absence of personal initiative even among her cultured minority, a conservatory would do much more harm on Russian soil than in Western Europe. Rubinstein had erred, Stasov felt, in taking as his norm the vigorous "bottom-up" musical culture of the German States, where every hamlet had its own choir and philharmonia. In the vast, underdeveloped Russian Empire, where progress had always been enforced from the top down, an official institution would merely breed more careerists. Russian writers had never been officially licensed, but what miracles had come to pass in literature! Diplomas, medals, and bestowed status would not benefit the cause of Russian music.

Stasov's next point cuts to the core of Musorgsky's complaint about the "German professoriat," its "fixed pillars" inscribed with "idiotic scrawls" that pretend to be "musical laws" but that in fact only "infect students in advance." Artistic education is not like science, Stasov insists. Fields that investigate objective knowledge can be housed in universities. But a conservatory is not that sort of institution. It "interferes with the *creative process* of the artist in training, and thus wields a despotic power." Here, it seems, is the nub of the disagreement. In his article, Rubinstein had argued against amateurs in music because in his opinion only the full-time professional could "open himself up to universal criticism – without which he will never produce anything of greatness." But the creative process, Stasov (and with him, Musorgsky) would claim, both in nations and in individuals, could not be approached as a universal.

The implications of this position are wide-ranging. If music does not have "laws" of the sort that conservatory training imparts, what does it have? If one does not go to school to learn musical language and forms, from what mysterious source do a sense of form and the tools of one's trade emerge? What is appropriate preparatory activity for a serious musician? The Balakirev Circle only partially addressed these questions. The method Balakirev himself used with his "pupils" was imperiously one-on-one, a study of the scores of great composers followed by assignments and "corrections." The most gifted and original musical mind in the group aroused his impatience most quickly. When Musorgsky congratulated Balakirev in spring 1862 on his "newborn school," which had rejected the "professorial anti-musical togas" of the Germans in favor of a "free association of kindred spirits in art," he was referring to the Free Music School that had opened its doors in March of that year. The new school specialized in choral singing and elementary musical lessons for the general public, not in pre-professional training. Competition and personal hostility between these two very different institutions was hardly mandatory.

There were numerous family and avocational ties. The Russian Musical Society had sponsored Musorgsky's debut as a composer in January 1860, with his Scherzo in B♭, which went very well under Rubinstein's baton. Dmitry Stasov, lawyer and devoted younger brother of the more famous *kuchkist* spokesman Vladimir, was highly knowledgeable in music and served for many years on the board of directors of the Russian Musical Society; it was Dmitry who introduced Musorgsky's piece to Rubinstein. (Liudmila Shestakova, both matron and patroness to the Balakirev Circle, had been close to Dmitry Stasov before his marriage; he was the father of her daughter Olga.) Balakirev himself replaced Rubinstein as director of the Russian Musical Society in 1867, thus linking the two branches in his person and becoming one of the most influential figures in the music life of the capital. Granted that the Society was wealthier than the School, and that Balakirev did not endear himself to his German-bred colleagues in the Society's orchestra when he insisted on addressing them in Russian, still, did the battle lines Musorgsky drew in his letters to Balakirev have to be drawn in such an acerbic way?

With hardly a composition to his name and still bending obediently to Balakirev's assignments, the twenty-one-year-old Musorgsky was already raging against the Society. (The occasion was a planned performance of his chorus for *Oedipus*; in November 1860, displeased with the presentation, he took the chorus back, remarking to Balakirev: "Does this idiotic outfit really suppose it can teach me?" [L, 27]). Musorgsky did not take kindly to the systems of others. But being by temperament an accommodator in social situations, he tended to play to the prejudices of his interlocutors. As a rule, he did not offer positive general solutions. In an era when Russian intellectuals were busy correcting flawed institutions, writing textbooks, trying to make their country economically account-worthy, going public with their complaints, Musorgsky continued to "put his own brains in order." Music criticism from his pen was confined exclusively to personal letters. The only exception here were ripostes in the form of musical compositions. One, in 1867, was a satire song entitled "The Classic," sung to the tune of an injured eighteenth-century melody and directed against one Professor Famintsyn of the Conservatory, author of a hostile review of Rimsky-Korsakov's *Sadko*; another was a more ambitious, although musically insignificant, travesty against enemies of The Five called "The Peepshow." Amid these burgeoning music institutions, no one sought Musorgsky out as a teacher, except his friends or hosts who, on rare occasion, wanted elementary piano lessons for their children.

And as suggested by the supercilious comment in his letter to Balakirev on Rubinstein's concern with "finances and glory," Musorgsky remained in the high-aristocratic mold as regards money. He simply did not want to think about it. He wanted others to make it and manage it. Close attention to the cost of something, or a desire to be paid what one's labor is worth, was unattractively philistine. In January 1867 he wrote to Balakirev, then conducting Glinka's operas in Prague, a long disdainful letter against the high salaries the *allemands* were making at the Conservatory. His special target was "Tupinstein," "'wholly devoted' to the cause of music" but in fact "wishing to get rich out of the Russian pocket" (L, 79). In an attitude that was to move smoothly from the old-regime aristocracy into radical Bolshevik ideology, music – or any true value – was dishonored if it turned a profit or brought a living wage. It was more "Russian" to endure poverty with dignity, or to live at the expense of wealthy friends, than to make money and invest it thriftily. Accountants were "German," like Goncharov's efficient and thrifty Stolz.

For all the conventional wisdom that has placed Musorgsky among the populists of his generation, therefore, we must conclude – however this goes against the grain of his time – that he was not a practical or public-spirited man. In his personal letters, he was as discomfited by the necessity to seek patrons as he was by the official procedures being drafted for the licensing and salarying of music schools. Intensely focused on his own development and eclectic in his musical feedings, he relied upon his phenomenal individual gifts to propel himself forward: mastery of the keyboard, a perfect ear, an improvisatory imagination of the genius caliber, an ability to recall in full harmonic complexity whole stretches of music after a single hearing, and, of course, a stubborn and tenacious intellect. Larger social reformations left him indifferent. And for the time being, the "study circle" approach to musical production continued to satisfy his needs.

At its most densely scheduled during these years, the group gathered somewhere in St. Petersburg almost every evening. It met on Mondays and Fridays at Liudmila Shestakova's, Wednesdays at Balakirev's, Thursdays at Dargomyzhsky's, Saturdays at the Opochinins', and Sundays at Stasov's. Memoir accounts of Musorgsky at these musical gatherings, which continued in some form up through the mid-1870s, are radiant. He played, sang in his expressive baritone, did dramatic readings, befriended his hosts' young children (who were enraptured by him), all better than anyone else. During 1867, however, there was a change in tone at these soirées. This was due in part to a shift in the musical politics of the capital, after Rubinstein resigned as director of the Russian Musical Society and Balakirev was appointed his successor. To fill his concert program, the new director wanted symphonic works from his former

11 Musorgsky at the piano with Nikolai Rubinstein, Anton's younger brother and
    director of the Moscow Conservatory

pupils. It was a triumphant moment: after a decade of mentoring (and sometimes measure by measure) the work of his protégés, Balakirev was at last in a position to sponsor them to the wider public. But the "pupils," as we saw in the scandal with Modest's witches, were breaking free. Not only Musorgsky but also Rimsky-Korsakov pulled at the leash. Both were experimenting in texted music (songs and operas) rather than in the instrumental genres Balakirev needed. Both felt more comfortable at Dargomyzhsky's, especially since the older composer was just beginning his word-for-word setting of Pushkin's "little tragedy" on the Don Juan theme, *The Stone Guest*. For the mighty little heap of nationalist composers, the "Balakirev evenings" had now become only one class – and an elective at that – in a much more differentiated school.

After leaving the commune, Modest spent the next three years as a member of his elder brother's household. During the summers they moved to Minkino, a village still in Filaret's possession, where the outdoor life with its jam-making, bathing, long walks, and light farming was good tonic for Modest's constitution. Winters were spent in the apartment of Filaret and his wife in St. Petersburg. Except for a brief period of unemployment after April 1867, the younger brother clerked afternoons at the Engineering Authority. Thus, up until 1868 – by which time the family's income had so diminished that Filaret was forced to relinquish his town property and settle permanently in the countryside – there was (so to speak) a steady "Agafya Matveyevna" component in Musorgsky's life in St. Petersburg. He had a home, a stimulating circle of colleagues, and he could think and work. His unsuspected musical originality began to manifest itself.

In the fall of 1866, after a summer in Minkino, Musorgsky brought the earliest of his so-called "realistic songs" to show his colleagues in St. Petersburg. Two of them, "Gopak" and "Svetik Savishna," were published in 1867. It was his first mature work to be so recognized. How did these songs, and the more ambitious text-setting embarked upon in the following year, embody the "laws" and "forms" to which

Musorgsky felt music should be true? How did he intend to turn these principles into a fully elaborated musical language? Musorgsky's aesthetic aims during this period have been called "realistic," but the attribute is highly unsatisfactory for a medium such as music. "Real" in the sense of faithful to some mimetic imitation or "natural truth" was never part of the composer's project. "Realist" in the special sense the term enjoyed in late nineteenth-century Russia and France – namely, a preference among writers and artists for themes or images that are naturalistic, everyday, down to earth, even ugly – is perhaps closer to the mark. In his art songs, Musorgsky did avoid elevated love themes in favor of fishwives, beggars, philandering young women, village idiots, orphans, and very small children. But his realism was differently motivated from that of his populist contemporaries, being less lachrymosely sentimental, less political, more "organic" and scientific.

A letter to Stasov several years later (October 1872) pinpoints this difference, drawing on evolutionary biology. In this letter, Musorgsky, enthusiastic over his recent reading of Darwin, credits that great natural scientist with "confirming his most ardent dream," that "the artistic depiction of beauty alone, in its material sense, is sheer childishness – art in its infancy" (L, 199). Implied here are two related principles that might indeed be understood loosely as "Darwinian." Once embraced by Musorgsky, they put him at the far edge of musical practice as understood in the Russia of his time.

The first principle is *process*: a celebration of the very fact of transition, of possible movement in multiple directions that is independent of beginnings and ends. Carried to its most exuberant extreme, processual writing would postpone closure, subvert full cadence, blur or avoid musical sectionalism, undermine functional harmony by opening it up, increase tonal ambiguity – with the result, in the words of one advocate, that "Musorgsky does not so much hide meaning, as refuse to delimit meaning."[5] The closeness of this credo to Wagnerian ideas is startling, given the hostility on the part of the *kuchkist* composers to their great German contemporary. Musorgsky had other means for accomplishing this task, but he sensed Wagner's daring and respected it. "We often abuse Wagner," he wrote Rimsky-Korsakov in September 1867, "but Wagner is powerful, powerful in that he lays his hands on art and yanks it around. If he were more talented, he would do much more" (L, 101).

A second principle follows from processual writing: non-predetermination or *surprise*. In a world where all aspects of the environment are in flux, unexpected mutations keep living things alive for longer than would be possible under a more absolutist reign of established rules or formulas. These two principles are not, of course, opposed to laws per se. But they are opposed to the sort of *universal* laws (or criticism) that Rubinstein considered essential for the serious professional practitioner of music. In the same 1867 letter to Rimsky mentioned above, Musorgsky added a postscript, presumptuous as well as generous: "Overlooking the faults of the above-mentioned leaders in musical matters [Wagner, Berlioz, Liszt], which are hidden and occasionally protrude, the works themselves will never die in the historical evolution of art and will always be bright points of intelligent artistic creation . . ." In his third-person autobiographical sketch from 1880, he repeats this sentiment and links it to the proper understanding of laws. Poignantly, it is the last full sentence, after which the manuscript breaks off: "Acknowledging that in the realm of art only artist-reformers such as Palestrina, Bach, Gluck, Beethoven, Berlioz and Liszt have created the laws of art, he considers these laws are not immutable but liable to change and progress, like the entire spiritual world of man."

That the principles of process and surprise were central to Musorgsky early on and opposed in his mind to the "fixed scrawls" taught to conservatory students is evident from his correspondence over a wide period. He internalized these ideas from his first lessons with Balakirev, and they continued to trigger in him a sort of ecstasy. In an excited letter to Rimsky-Korsakov in July 1867, he wrote:

My dear and kind Korsinka, on the twenty-third of June on St. John's
Eve, with God's help, was finished St. John's Night on Bald Mountain
[his "witches"] . . . The general character of the thing is hot; it
doesn't drag, the transitions are compact and dense without any
Germanic approach, which really freshens things up . . . In my
opinion, "St. John's Eve" is something new and should make a
satisfactory impression on the thinking musician. (L, 85, 87)

Or put another way, his "witches" were to appeal to the emotions,
which were reached through the mind. In Musorgsky's view, keeping
up mental interest was a matter of devising unusual connective tissue,
exploiting a common tone for an unconventional progression. This
freshness and hotness would in turn fulfill the function that, in more
static or obedient aesthetic systems, is accomplished by beauty.

Here we glimpse a reason for Musorgsky's uneasy reception of his
exact contemporary and rival, the conservatory-trained Tchaikovsky.
Musorgsky played *The Nursery* and the Inn Scene from *Boris* for
Tchaikovsky during a soirée at Cui's in December 1872; he reports
drily that Tchaikovsky dozed through both. And Tchaikovsky, while
expressing some admiration for the sheer boldness of Musorgsky's
writing, was frank in his disgust for musicians who dragged "truth"
into the sphere of art. The two had little to say to each other.
Musorgsky wrote to Stasov immediately after that evening:

I've had to spend all these days in the company of worshipers of
absolute musical beauty. And I have experienced a strange *feeling
of emptiness* in conversation with them. This strange feeling of
emptiness was replaced by an even stranger one, but the feeling was
not to be put off – and I cannot name it: it is the sort of feeling one
experiences upon losing a very near and dear person . . . (L, 200)

Absolute beauty as predictability, predictability as stasis, and
stasis as loss and death: the composer was on guard against this tri-
partite sequence throughout his life. Thus are his harmonic textures
so often not obedient. And thus did the mature Rimsky-Korsakov
(who turned somewhat in Tchaikovsky's direction in his later career)

despair over his friend's "terrible voice-leading" and strive after 1881 to rewrite it, because the subordinate parts had forgotten their role in the hierarchy and had been allowed to misbehave. How poignant, in a way, that it was precisely to Rimsky-Korsakov that Musorgsky wrote in August 1868, encouraging him to compose boldly in a "Korsakov manner" instead of a Schumann one. "Oh, preliminaries!" he wrote to his friend. "How many good things they have ruined! . . . The German, when he thinks, first theorizes at length, and then proves; our Russian brother proves first, and then amuses himself with theory" (L, 120–21).

But any liberating device too often indulged becomes either anarchy or a tedious convention of its own. In Musorgsky's practice, declamatory freedom and a bold sort of functional harmony continually interrupt and relieve one another. For the prerogative – or the illusion – of unexpected movement, irregularity, imbalance, was precious to him. It figured in his minimal conditions for a true "conversation" (among tones or among speakers). "Art is a means for conversing with people": let us recall that quotation from 1880 and the questions arising from it in the preface, amplifying them somewhat here. In artistic conversation, what qualifies as an autonomous voice? Must there be someone out there listening to that voice and poised to answer it? In a musically set conversation, are questions (which expect answers) rendered differently from statements or commands (which do not), or jokes (which, if they are not to fall flat, require a zone of shared laughter)? Why would a "thinking musician" wish to apprentice himself to the task of notating conversation, with all its caprice and surprise? Musorgsky's vocal compositions from 1866 to 1868 tackle these issues head on. About twenty songs survive from this period, the best of which are "realistic" (including the initial song in the *Nursery* cycle); there are also the terminally prosaic scenes he set from Gogol's *Marriage*. Although received with varying degrees of enthusiasm (Stasov was rapturous; Balakirev, profoundly put off), these vocal experiments in the "conversational mode" placed Musorgsky beyond the pale of the Balakirev Circle for good. Several of these works took their impetus from real-life scenes, others are biographically meaningful for other reasons. But even the most naturalistic of these vocal settings are profoundly shaped. None are naive transcription.

One such composition is the early song, "Svetik Savishna" [Darling Savishna]. Stasov has left us a version of its genesis. "Musorgsky himself told me the story back then, he thought up the song while he was in the country at his brother's farm at Minkino in the summer of 1865," Stasov writes.

> Once he was standing by the window and was struck by some clamor going on below. An unfortunate village idiot was declaring his love to a young peasant woman who had attracted him; he was pleading with her, although at the same time he was ashamed of himself, his ugliness and his unhappy condition; he himself understood that nothing in the world existed for him, least of all the happiness of love. Musorgsky was deeply struck by all this; the type and the scene fixed themselves in his mind, original forms and sounds for embodying the images that had so shaken him appeared to him in a flash. But he didn't write down the song at that moment ... only after several months did he finish "Savishna."[6]

Stasov's account is naive – if only for its image of Musorgsky as a "naive" artist, effortlessly keeping a diary in sounds. Its more likely genesis and genre are more complex. For "Svetik Savishna" is neither lyrical nor recitative but some third thing alien to both. In forty-seven measures of uninterrupted, rhythmically unchanging *moto perpetuo* modules in 5/4 time ("no place at all to breathe," was the irritated reaction of César Cui, to whom the song was dedicated), the singer-idiot limps after the village beauty, trying to communicate his love and conceal his shame. So limited are his expressive means and so damaged is his wit that good news and bad, passion and blame, all emerge in the same stylized, uniform intonation. The song cuts off abruptly, as if the hopelessness of the situation suddenly becomes clear to him and he falls behind – and falls silent. This is a conversation (the girl is present, addressed, physically pursued) but one that is so needy, and needy in such an undifferentiated way, that the aloneness of the feeble-minded singer remains at the end the overwhelming image. One can see how Stasov arrived at his sympathetic mimetic reading. But "Svetik Savishna" (as Richard Taruskin has argued) is at the furthest possible pole from spontaneous, naturalistic, "prosy" art. The verbal text, which Musorgsky himself composed, is cast in the highly stylized meter of a peasant wedding song. The idiot sings of an unreality, in the one genre he knows he will never realize in his own life.[7] "A ghastly scene, Shakespeare in music," the music critic and opera composer Alexander Serov remarked upon hearing it, grasping this "acted" component.[8] After 1867, Musorgsky would on occasion write letters to his favorite interlocutors (Liudmila Shestakova among them) in the voice and persona of Savishna, one of his most tantalizing epistolary masks.

A less painful, more straightforward example of musical conversation is the first of the Nursery songs, "With Nanny," which Musorgsky composed (words and music) in 1868. It is as healthy, integrated, and spontaneous an illustration of the eagerly communicating psyche as "Svetik Savishna" is lonely and disoriented. Six more songs were added to the cycle, four in 1870 and two in 1872 (with an additional two worked out on the keyboard but never written down). These seven bright "conversations of childhood" are unusual in the literature of music for children. They are not songs *to* children sung by grownups (as are lullabies) nor are they nostalgic songs *about* childhood sung by adults. They more resemble the sort of song that children themselves might compose about their experiences, had they the technical skills to do so. Musorgsky, who intensely loved children, treated them seriously and felt completely at ease with them; and he was adored by them in turn. He tried out these little vocal scenes on his nephew and niece as well as on the toddlers of his friends. Their understanding was immediate and enthusiastic.

The Nursery is a collage of scenes that take place entirely in an active present tense. A little boy is frightened by a fairy tale or scolded by his nanny for knocking her ball of yarn to the floor; outside at play, he is

12   Portrait of Musorgsky, 1865

startled by a huge beetle and runs to tell his mother; he falls off a hobby-horse and must be soothed before he can gallop away; he watches while a cat tries to nab a canary in a cage; a little girl says her prayers and sings her dolly to sleep. Musorgsky wrote the words (or rather, "overheard the words") himself. Equipped with a strip of uttered children's dialogue, he would set to work on pitch intervals, amplifying the intonation curve into a melodic line and registering doubts, anxieties, and sudden pleasure in phrasing and pauses. The pulse of the first song, "With Nanny," is almost untranscribable; time signatures change with every measure. The aim was to avoid fitting words into music or music into words, but rather to experience both parameters as a single continuum, with neither component felt to be under constraint. The song is thus not actually "performed" (in the sense of "recalled experience," the ideal of a lyric romance) as much as it is *enacted*. "Whatever speech I hear, no matter who is speaking (or what the person is speaking about), my brain immediately sets to working out a musical exposition for this speech," Musorgsky wrote to Rimsky-Korsakov in July 1868 (L, 113). The task is demanding because no two utterances are ever alike. Although he did later relax this rule (the final two songs in *Nursery*, composed several years later, are evidence of it), among the composers of his circle Musorgsky was the least willing to exploit music's tolerance for lyrical repetition. Here is a third principle that may be added to the composer's evolving sense of "musical realism." He valued not just process and surprise (lessons that he absorbed from Balakirev and then confirmed in evolutionary biology), but the necessity for accurate *individuation*. By the summer of 1868, this aspect of his musical art had come to occupy Musorgsky more than any other. "Accuracy in psychological expression" became the ideal in his highly unconventional setting of the opening scenes of Gogol's play *Marriage*.

Before we consider that curious project, however, it is important to see Musorgsky's development in the context of his musical colleagues. By the end of the 1860s, many of them (in belated confirmation of Rubinstein's mournful prediction for amateur musicians) were turning their attentions to opera. This was not, of course, the tuneful Italian-style opera that had long dominated the big theatres of St. Petersburg; that craze, with its diva-mania, had gone into a decline, even though box-office receipts and the high fees paid to Italian composers, companies, and leading stars remained a sore point with Russian musicians.[9] Nor was there any sympathy among The Five for a Wagnerian "reform" of the genre. Knowledge of Wagner's operas – and even more, of his polemical writings – was scant in the Russian capital, except for isolated enthusiasts such as Alexander Serov. (In October 1868, Dargomyzhsky, Balakirev, Musorgsky, and Rimsky-Korsakov took a box in the Imperial Opera House in St. Petersburg for the opening night of *Lohengrin*. According to Rimsky in his memoirs, all four greeted the opera with contempt; Cui even wrote a coarse review entitled "Lohengrin, or Curiosity Punished.") There were, however, some operatic composers whom the Russian nationalists did respect, Mikhail Glinka above all. Inspired by Glinka's example, by 1868 most of the Circle had come to believe that Russian literature and themes deserved to be taken with high seriousness.

Topics and texts were literally handed around to possible takers, with Stasov, again, the most energetic provisioner. Borodin, soon to be caught up in his *Prince Igor*, began and then abandoned an Ivan-the-Terrible opera on Lev Mey's drama *The Tsar's Bride* (much later, Rimsky-Korsakov would take over the theme). Even Balakirev, despite his preference for orchestral genres, contemplated setting Chernyshevsky's *What Is To Be Done*, as well as an opera on *The Fire-Bird*. Dargomyzhsky, by now in very poor health but perhaps in part for that reason a reinvigorated influence on the younger musicians, was passionately occupied with his setting of *The Stone Guest*. His goal was to embody Pushkin's miniature drama faithfully in musical form without altering a single word; his motto, "truth in music," meant to him a continuous, malleable arioso-style "musicking" of a received poetic text. Of all the group's activities, Dargomyzhsky's experiment with Pushkin was the closest to Musorgsky's flexible practice in his first

Nursery song. It was to Dargomyzhsky that Musorgsky dedicated
"With Nanny" – and the older man, upon hearing it, remarked with
gratitude that Musorgsky in this song had already "gone beyond."

Just how far beyond would become very clear in *Marriage*.
Dargomyzhsky was intent upon preserving and musically amplifying
Pushkin's words. But *The Stone Guest* was already an elegant, compact
text by the greatest poet in the Russian language. To realize it honestly
in music meant to reflect the text's own lyricism and impeccable balance; thus, the opera's most successful musical episodes begin as
phrases conditioned by a portion of verbal text and then develop lyri-
cally, in the manner of a through-composed romance. In contrast,
Gogol's 1843 drama *Marriage* is aggressively anti-lyrical. It is written
in colloquial prose that is consciously stripped of poetic dignity, both
in diction and in theme. What the play has in abundance is highly personalized, often quite unpredictable, talk. It was this quality that
seized Musorgsky. In a letter to Rimsky-Korsakov in July 1868 he
wrote: "I have looked over my work – it is interestingly carried out –
however, who knows . . . I am on trial. I'll say just this one thing: if one
completely renounces operatic traditions and visualizes musical dialogue on the stage as just ordinary conversation, then *Marriage* is an
opera" (L, 113).

There is much in Gogol's odd little story that must have appealed to
Musorgsky. It is, after a fashion, the prototypical Oblomov plot.
Deeds are not allowed to get in the way. The hero Podkolyosin, a bachelor and functionary, is lying on the couch as the curtain rises.
Nothing is happening. He wants nothing to happen. But he thinks
that something should: "When you start thinking things through like
this, at your leisure, you do come to feel that, after all, one has to . . .
marriage is the only way. What else is there, after all? You live and you
live, and in the end you just can't take it any longer. Now I've gone and
missed the marrying season again . . ."[10] This monologue constitutes
almost the whole of scene 1. Podkolyosin calls in his servant and quiz-
zes him on his frockcoat at the tailor's, on the shoe polish, but by the
time the matchmaker arrives he is still supine and in indecision.

Finally, one of his married friends coaxes him into visiting the bridal candidate; unfortunately, five other suitors turn up at the same time and the prospective bride cannot make up her mind. The friend presses a strong suit for Podkolyosin. The bride is persuaded and leaves the room to don her wedding dress; the bridegroom, having just congratulated himself on finally securing the marriage, jumps out the window and escapes.

Every voice in this drama is hesitant, blustering, or insincere. What characters *say* is much richer and more conflicted than what they actually *do*; "doing," in fact, has a very small role in the play. Gogol is a goldmine of inflection. Thus it was the perfect raw material through which Musorgsky could study the twistings and turnings of the individuated utterance. As he wrote Cui at the beginning of July 1868, his *opéra dialogué* was an attempt "to outline as closely as possible those changes in intonation which occur in the actors during dialogue, apparently for the most trivial reasons and on the most insignificant words; in this, or so it seems to me, is hidden the power of Gogol's humor" (L, 109). Musorgsky literally assigned himself, as Balakirev used to do for him, this work on *Marriage*. With academic severity, rhythmic periods are avoided, tonal motion remains static, intervals are all but unsingable, and choppy paralexical detail reflecting anxiety, frustration, and irritation obstruct any musical segmentation.[11] After a sing-through at Dargomyzhsky's, Rimsky-Korsakov remarked that the group was amazed – but at the same time perplexed at some of the chords and harmonic progressions. Borodin, writing to his wife in Moscow at the end of September, called it curious, paradoxical, full of innovations and great humor, but "as a whole – *une chose manquée*" (L, 124). Perhaps Musorgsky agreed; in any event, he abandoned it after he had learned the necessary skills. What, then, had been the larger goal?

The answer, I believe, lies in Musorgsky's intense curiosity about the interplay of freedom and necessity. This philosophical question, like the problem of the verbal utterance, was an area in which the musical disciplines had something important to contribute to human knowledge. Music too could be a laboratory science; text-settings by "thinking musicians" could be "experiments." Musorgsky's passion for Darwin, let us recall, was in part his realization to what extent human beings are "caught in a vise" – and he hastened to add just how pleasant, oddly pleasant, it was to be in that vise, by which he meant (we might assume) in intellectual possession of the rules that govern us. His 1880 autobiography insists that "human speech is strictly controlled by musical laws."

Musorgsky attributes this article of faith to two eminent German scholars: Rudolf Virchow (1821–1902), anthropologist, social activist, and cellular pathologist; and Georg Gottfried Gervinus (1805–71), Shakespeare scholar and aesthetician. Gervinus's 1868 book on Händel, Shakespeare, and the art of intonation was an important stimulus to the rigors and subtleties involved in setting *Marriage*. But the Germans whom Musorgsky so admired were content to be analytical scientists. In contrast, the Russians' passion for science during this polemical decade – as their passion for so much else in the world of human values – was not merely pursuit of knowledge or precision. There was a strong utopian element as well. If Pavlov's laboratory dogs succumbed to conditioning, perhaps the human being too would submit to external laws. Some nineteenth-century thinkers (most famously, Dostoevsky) feared this possibility and fought it like the plague; Musorgsky, however, was no Dostoevsky in this regard. In his view, inductive science, if brought to bear on the uttered word, could bring a type of salvation; it could teach us how to think and *why* we think the way we do. The human being is the highest organism, Musorgsky confided in mid-August 1868 to his friend, the historian Vladimir Nikolsky. Knowledge is not hostile to freedom. If one could "catch the intonations of the human voice in art . . . and, at the same time, capture the thinking processes as well: wouldn't that be a worthy occupation?" (L, 122).

The ultimate purpose of conversation, then, was to "tune up" one's own thought. Perhaps this was the end Musorgsky had in mind when he wrote to Shestakova, in July 1868, that "my music must be an artistic reproduction of human speech in all its finest shades, the *sounds of human speech* as the external manifestation of thought and feeling . . . true, accurate music, but artistic, highly artistic! . . . *Marriage* is a cage, in which I am imprisoned until I am tamed, but afterwards – to freedom" (L, 114, 113). Several weeks later he expressed the same idea in a letter to Rimsky-Korsakov (L, 121), but this time ventriloquized through the words of Podkolyosin. These words open both Gogol's play and his own operatic setting of it. " 'When you start thinking things through like this, at your leisure, you do come to feel that, after all, one has to . . .' " and then Musorgsky broke off and added in his own voice: "become one's own self."

4 1868–1874: Musorgsky and Russian history

By the summer of 1868, Musorgsky had acquired the discipline, experience, and musical vocabulary to begin "becoming his own self." As he wrote to Liudmila Shestakova, he was ready to exit the "cage" of *Marriage* into creative freedom. Curiously, the first steps toward this self-realization are almost completely unrecorded. That autumn, Musorgsky moved in with the Opochinins, brother and sister, who provided him with warm friendship, highly musical surroundings, and solicitous composing space. Neither the composer nor his gracious hosts left any recollections of the period. From August 1868 – the month Gogol's text was abandoned in favor of Pushkin's drama *Boris Godunov* – to May 1870, by which time *Boris* was finished in its first version, there are no extant letters except for one trifling note to Balakirev. In contrast with his earlier practice, the composer played only fragments of the emerging project to his own circle (Dargomyzhsky heard the Inn Scene before his death in January 1869). Apparently he did not write about the new opera at all.

Musorgsky was no longer seeking musical advice. He was also kept busy, and quite possibly worn down, by his clerking duties. Laid off from the Central Engineering Authority in the spring of 1867 and unable to do without a salary, he found employment in December 1868 as assistant chief in the Forestry section of the Ministry of State Domains, a position he was to hold for a decade. It was not a sinecure; some two dozen bundles of documents in Musorgsky's fastidious handwriting were discovered in the archives of the department. But other written traces of this period are few. What memoir accounts we have – most of which discuss Musorgsky's "ordeal" with the Imperial Theatre Directorate – begin with the year 1870 and are inconsistent, unreliable, and self-serving. The composer is portrayed as recalcitrant, the Directorate as hostile and malign. Although the five "Boris years" constitute the peak of Musorgsky's public life, their accurate telling has required careful reconstructive work.[1]

The idea for an opera based on Pushkin's 1825 drama was given to Musorgsky by his friend Vladimir Nikolsky, historian and Pushkinist. (Stasov, endearingly, admitted to being deeply chagrined that he had not been the source.) Work went forward at astonishing speed: the piano-vocal score – seven of Pushkin's twenty-five scenes, set as modified *opéra dialogué* – was complete by July 1869 and the orchestration in place by the end of December. Unlike Pushkin's play, and unlike Musorgsky's own later revision of the opera, Dmitry the Pretender was allotted only two scenes in this initial version. (With his exotic biography and Polish amours, Dmitry had been a dominant figure in previous artistic treatments of the story.) Instead, Musorgsky set three types of scene: comic episodes, extended narrative monologue, and episodes illustrating Boris's ambition, bitterness, and psychological torment. The choice is significant, for the composer's initiation into Russian history and historical opera was not through the familiar Sentimentalist, Romantic, or patriotic venues. His entry was through Gogol, and – appropriately for this plot of murder, guilt, and punishment – through the rising literary star of the 1860s, Dostoevsky. As in *Marriage*, precise musical expression of individual psychology was crucial to Musorgsky. But Pushkin's characters had psyches far more complex and multifaceted than Gogol's hilarious slapstick cast. To tell their tragedy, skills of a different subtlety were required. In any event, the broad social panoramas usually considered central to historical drama would come only later.

Musorgsky submitted his opera to the Directorate of the Imperial Theatres in the fall of 1870. At the time, there was no other route to public performance. Since 1803, theatres in the Russian Empire had been a crown monopoly administered directly by the civil bureaucracy (this monopoly would last until 1882, a year after Musorgsky's death, at which time private theatres funded by the new industrial magnates assumed cultural leadership). Although St. Petersburg had four imperial theatres in the 1870s, only one, the Maryinsky, performed Russian works. Not surprisingly, competition was stiff.[2] In February 1871, *Boris Godunov* was formally rejected. From a box-office perspective, the grounds were plausible: there was no prima donna role. The opera's other irregular aspects (a *parlando* text setting, the seemingly *ad hoc* harmony) were apparently less offensive to the review committee than its lack of all those familiar spectacles and conventional episodes – ensembles, dances, love duets – that were known to please a theatre audience. Musorgsky immediately began to revise, changing much more than required by the Directorate.

Musorgsky was immensely excited by the revisions. His stalled correspondence resumed; for the first time, he became concerned about performance considerations beyond a chamber setting. After one play-through, in July 1870, of several scenes from *Boris* before a large group of friends, he wrote to Rimsky-Korsakov expressing astonishment that "some found it to be *bouffe* (!), others perceived tragedy" (L, 148). This would not do; he would seek new devices to elevate the opera's tone, ensure seriousness even in the comically dialogic choruses, link psychology with destiny through musical motifs, and make tragedy plausible on the *historical* – as well as the personal – plane.[3] A Polish act, already drafted, was revived and stitched in to provide the necessary love interest, divertissements, and interpolated dances. As additional relief from stretches of uninterrupted recitative, Musorgsky inserted folk songs, duets, laments, and children's prattle. But he resisted what other composers of historical opera during these decades (for example, Rimsky-Korsakov and Tchaikovsky) would not resist: a Western-style romantic love plot attached to events in medieval Muscovy. On this point Musorgsky remained faithful to Pushkin, who himself had been faithful to history. Chivalric courtship was out of place on Old Russian soil. "True love" is difficult to find even in the Polish scenes, where Marina Mniszech, in both play and opera, is cold and openly motivated by political ambition. This unsentimental aspect of Pushkin appealed to the highly intellectual Musorgsky, for whom the role of lover, as we have seen, was neither natural nor compatible with his temperament.

The biggest change in the opera was the addition of a new final scene. Quite likely it was triggered by a shift in living arrangements. In the fall of 1871, Musorgsky and Rimsky-Korsakov decided to rent a furnished room. "This, I imagine, is the only instance of two composers living together," Rimsky wrote in his memoirs.

> How could we help being in each other's way? This is how we managed. Mornings until about noon, Musorgsky used the piano, and I did copying or else orchestrated something fully thought out. By noon he would go to his departmental duties, leaving the piano at my disposal . . . That autumn and winter the two of us accomplished a good deal, with constant exchange of ideas and plans. Musorgsky composed and orchestrated the Polish Act of *Boris Godunov* and the people's scene "Near Kromy." I orchestrated and finished my *Maid of Pskov*.[4]

Their friend Borodin concurred about the mutual benefits. "Modinka and Korsinka, since they have begun to share a room, have both greatly developed," Borodin wrote to his wife at the end of October 1871. "Modest has improved the recitative and declamatory sides of Korsinka who has, in his turn, wiped out Modest's tendency toward awkward originality" (L, 175). The "exchange of ideas" that Rimsky mentions very likely included Musorgsky's decision, made under the influence of the skillfully managed mass scenes that Rimsky was creating for *The Maid of Pskov*, to supplement his own opera with an insurrectionary scene, "Near Kromy," after the death of Boris.[5] With the addition of this episode, *Boris Godunov* moved from a drama of individual guilt to a statement about history and Russian destiny.

It was to be the last wholly successful musical co-mentoring in Musorgsky's life. In June 1872, Rimsky-Korsakov moved out and married. The Balakirev circle fell apart that year as well. The next eighteen months were lonely for Musorgsky. But the Boris revisions were finished that spring and, within a month after Rimsky's marriage, Musorgsky had already sketched and dated a plan for a second historical opera, to be called Khovanshchina. In July he wrote enthusiastically to Stasov, to whom he dedicated the plan of the (scarcely launched) new opera: "I lived Boris in Boris . . . Now the new work, your work, will boil, I am already beginning to live in it" (L, 194). Here was a man who, if minimally provisioned, could quickly create quarters in which to live.

When exactly the revised Boris was accepted by the Imperial Theatre Directorate is not certain, although most likely this occurred in May 1872. There is no evidence that it was rejected a second time, despite the persistence of that rumor in the Musorgsky martyrology. There were, of course, the usual bureaucratic delays, the intervention of Lent, summer holidays, prior commitments, the expense of a new production – but no special prejudice can be assumed against Musorgsky or the nationalist composers. (During the same period, Anton Rubinstein's opera The Demon was subject to even longer delays, in part due to church censorship, which balked at the representation of an evil spirit on stage.[6]) In February 1873, three scenes from Boris were successfully mounted at the Maryinsky Theatre; one year later, at end of January 1874, came the full premiere.

Musorgsky participated in all rehearsals and was deeply gratified by the production, even though the scene in Pimen's cell was omitted. Costumes and sets were lavish, having been recycled from the 1870 premiere of Pushkin's Boris Godunov (written in 1825, the drama was cleared for the stage only in 1866, three decades after its author's death). The premiere of the play had been a qualified failure. In the "realist-populist" 1860s and 1870s, the aristocratic poet Pushkin was out of vogue; he enjoyed nothing like the delirious cult that began to develop around him in the 1880s and has lasted until our present day. In fact, many progressively minded people wondered at Musorgsky's choice of so inauspicious a playwright and so austere a

13 Shishkov's stage design for the Inn Scene in the stage premiere of Pushkin's *Boris Godunov*, 1870

play as the literary base for his libretto. The composer was denounced by some critics for diluting the genius of Pushkin, but more often he was credited with rescuing an unstageworthy text. The opera sold out and was a great popular success.

The *Boris Godunov* plot was one of Europe's favorites. It was as riddled with historical legend as that of England's King Richard III. At the end of the sixteenth century, this ill-starred Russian tsar began his career as the trusted and progressive advisor to his brother-in-law Tsar Fyodor, Ivan the Terrible's feeble successor and second son (the first had been killed by his father in a fit of rage). When Tsar Fyodor died childless, the ancient dynasty came to an end. Although not of royal blood, Boris, by far the most competent contender, became tsar; he was crowned in 1598 and ruled successfully for several years. Then came a spell of floods, an unnatural frost in August, crop failure, and plague. Seeking scapegoats, the people blamed the "illegitimate" Tsar Boris for this withdrawal of God's grace. Gregory Otrepiev, an ambitious novice from a Moscow monastery, turned confusion to his advantage by claiming to be Tsarevich Dmitry, youngest son of Ivan the Terrible, who in 1591 had died in the provincial town of Uglich at the age of nine. In 1602, this "False Dmitry" fled to Catholic Poland, alleged that he had miraculously escaped Boris's attempt on his life in Uglich a decade earlier, recruited Jesuits to his cause, affianced himself to the Polish princess Marina Mniszech, and in 1604 attacked Muscovy with the support of disaffected Russian peasants. Much to his own surprise, his troops advanced rapidly. Boris died in 1605 as the False Dmitry was marching on Moscow. Once victorious, the Pretender's troops murdered Boris's widow and young reigning son, setting his daughter aside as a concubine for Dmitry. Dmitry's brief reign ushered in the seven years of foreign invasion, ghastly civil war, and famine known in Russian history as the *Smuta*, literally the "Darkening" or "Time of Troubles."

This was the story, sanctioned by the Russian chronicles, that Pushkin told in his play. Musorgsky copied it. It mattered little that the historical Boris was most likely not guilty of the death of the Tsarevich

Dmitry, or that a medieval Russian tsar, even if responsible for such an act, would never have died of "guilt" for a simple act of political expediency. The plot had become a staple of Romantic lore. Its earliest dramatic setting had been by the Spanish playwright Lope de Vega, in 1606, while the Smuta still raged; its most famous was by Schiller (his fragment Demetrius) in 1805. This Russian tale of intrigue and pretendership gained new meaning in the post-Napoleonic period, when it was utilized as a morality lesson against upstart, illegitimate political climbers who wished to make their way through bloodshed toward a throne not their own. Pushkin might have seemed an odd, old-fashioned choice as Musorgsky's intermediary text (the composer was his own librettist and adapted the drama skillfully). But the Boris tale itself was completely in the mainstream, both deeply Russian and pan-European.

Two disappointments marred the overall triumph of the Boris premiere. About the first, Musorgsky was too proud to complain, but it hardly could have gone unnoticed by this financially strapped head clerk in the Ministry of State Domains. His composer's fee for Boris, the fruit of five years' work, was 125 rubles per performance (assuming a sold-out house), or a little under $100. It was, of course, the first work by an untried author. Such compensation was within the legal norm for Russian opera, which had its own pay scale. (Italians were another matter; the Russian Imperial Theatres had paid Verdi almost $12,000 for the St. Petersburg premiere of his La forza del destino in 1862.) Twenty-one performances of Boris Godunov were given while Musorgsky was alive, from 1874 to 1879; his total income from them was just over $2,000.

About the second disappointment, the composer did complain. Although the opera was warmly received by its audience, reviews in print were mixed. Musorgsky had every reason to expect a cool reception from the conservative music camp. He indeed did suffer at the hands of Professor Famintsyn, whom he had lampooned so unkindly in his satire "The Classic." But otherwise he was faintly and pleasantly surprised. In 1873, Hermann Laroche, conservative music critic for

Golos [The Voice], had remarked that Musorgsky's art songs were so ugly and incoherent that, playing them through, he "always thought of the need to establish a corrective refuge for juvenile musical offenders."[7] In that same review, however, Laroche credited the three scenes from *Boris* mounted in 1873 with "originality and substance." His response to the full *Boris* a year later was also curiously positive. Like Rubinstein, Laroche disapproved of popular success in defiance of established rules. Such success could only set a disastrous, because infectious, precedent for less gifted amateurs. But Laroche admitted that Musorgsky, the most thorough "thinking realist" in Russian music, was a bold and gifted talent.

What Musorgsky did not expect – and bitterly resented – was a condescending review of his opera from his fellow *kuchkist* César Cui. Cui complimented the orchestration, some stretches of declamation, and the music of the Kromy scene. But in the tradition of Balakirev's old measure-by-measure method (that pedagogical technique which, we recall, the mature Rimsky-Korsakov found so offensive once he had outgrown it), Cui took potshots at separate parts, approving certain episodes, rejecting others, ignoring the shape of the whole. The opera is "rather like a potpourri," Cui wrote. Its defects were the result of "immaturity, of the fact that the composer does not criticize himself sharply enough, and of that unfastidious, self-satisfied, hasty process of composition that has led to such lamentable results in the cases of Messrs. Rubinstein and Tchaikovsky."[8]

The obscurity of César Cui as a composer lends this judgment, passed on two musical giants (and one highly competent "court composer"), a ludicrous ring today. Musorgsky, who was no stranger to caustic feedback from his own circle, could have waved the criticism aside. But *what* Cui chose to say, and in a public forum at that, stung him to the quick. He wrote to Stasov that same day: "What a horror that article of Cui's is! . . . and this reckless attack on the composer's self-satisfaction . . . Self-satisfaction! Hasty composition! Immaturity!! whose? . . . whose, I'd like to know?" (L, 266). It was not just that Cui misunderstood him musically. Creative musicians could differ about a work of art. It was the implied insult to his intellect. As we saw in the case of *Marriage*, Musorgsky prided himself on his quest for precision. His passion for Darwin and for positivist science grew out of his search for musical "laws." That a friend of so many years could accuse him of hastiness and lack of discipline was a painful blow.

Musorgsky was pleased to be a "thinking musician." During the *Boris* period, such aspirations on the part of artists were common. It was part of the spirit of the 1860s to rank products of the intellect over those of the heart, prose over poetry, mass social movements over soliloquy. Artworks were expected to be accessible and artists to be morally responsible. The populist intelligentsia endorsed the idea that progress was an inevitable law of human society; to document that law, progressive historians began to study the Russian population, with its vast sea of newly emancipated peasants, as scientific data with which to construct a new sense of Russian identity. In earlier periods, national history had meant "Caesarist" history, a mandatory account of the glory of tsars; now histories were written of serf revolts, religious dissenters, even of Russian taverns and drinking habits. When in 1871 Musorgsky added his Kromy scene to *Boris*, he was fully in step with his time.

Historical opera was taken very seriously during the reform era. It provided a user-friendly "textbook" of Russian options and potentials, despite the fact that censorship (secular and ecclesiastical) limited the scope of historical dramatists and restricted the lessons they could preach. Censorship had always been more severe for stage performance than for print. According to a decree of 1837, no member of the reigning House of Romanov could be portrayed on stage. The depiction of *pre*-Romanov tsars was permitted in "serious" tragedies and spoken historical dramas, but no tsar from any period could appear in opera. By the 1860s, this prohibition against "singing tsars" was being routinely waived. However, the stage ban on Romanovs (and on all canonized saints) remained in force, which made the final tsars of the prior dynasty and the interregnum (Ivan the Terrible through Boris Godunov, from the 1560s to 1612) very popular as dramatic protagonists. Working within these limits and respecting their role as educators to the nation, librettists and composers reflected specific schools of historical thought. Some followed the imperial or "statist" historians who believed, in Hegelian fashion, that Russia's "world-historical" time had finally arrived and deserved to be embellished with patriotic opera. Others were less sanguine – for the 1860s were a decade of nihilism as well as expansionism, in which negation and utopia competed for public favor. Musorgsky's two historical operas represent those two polar extremes, albeit in an original and highly spiritualized form.

For *Boris Godunov* embodies a strange vision of history, given the era in which it was composed. The opera's worldview is neither sentimental nor populist, nor is it in any sense imperialist. The insurrectionary energy of the Kromy scene is not sufficient to catapult us past its own grim ending – the holy fool's lament, predicting disaster for Russia. (Again, the finale of this opera more closely recalls Gogol's trademark of the stunned curtain and voided stage than it does the usual history in opera, such as Beethoven's *Fidelio* or the robust chorus that ends Glinka's *Ivan Susanin*.) In retrospect, the *Boris* premiere was prophetic, both in relation to Russian history and to Musorgsky's own biography. The year 1874 was a watershed for Russian populism. That summer, a bizarre event shook Russian society. Several thousand students and repentant aristocrats, dressed as peasants and trained as teachers, midwives, agricultural experts, and agitators, undertook a pilgrimage to the countryside to become, in their hopeful projection, "at one with the people." On the whole, village dwellers were suspicious and unresponsive; the regime was alarmed. With the peasants' help, two thousand arrests of populists were made, followed by mass trials. Directly on the heels of this debacle, the government – influenced by its own version of "historical inevitability," a rising tide of messianic pan-Slavism – went to war with Turkey. In the words of James Billington, among the most poetic scholars writing on this period: "This war gave Russian society and Russian social thought a feeling for violence and ideological fanaticism that made any return to the optimistic, evolutionary ideals of early populism extraordinarily difficult."9

Before considering this new climate and its great operatic issue, *Khovanshchina*, we must attend to some non-musical (or quasi-musical) events in the composer's life. They culminate in a non-event, which stretched throughout 1873: Musorgsky's failure to travel to Weimar and meet Franz Liszt. This negative decision came to mark Musorgsky – and can be seen as a symbolic divide. He would never leave Russia. He would not integrate himself (nor introduce himself personally) into the company of those modern Western musicians who had so shaped him in his youth. And he would begin to have something large and private to hide, even from his closest friends.

Musorgsky was slightly affiliated with a task that increasingly occupied the nationalist composers as their work began to be published in the early 1870s: acquainting Western Europe with their compositions. In 1873, Vasily Bessel (of Bessel & Company, the leading St. Petersburg music publisher) asked Musorgsky, whose German was excellent, to fit a German translation of Pushkin's drama *The Stone Guest* to Dargomyzhsky's score in preparation for its distribution abroad. The firm had begun to publish Musorgsky's music as well. Among famous European friends of Russian music, Liszt was the most enthusiastic – and in May 1873, Bessel made his first trip to Weimar to provide Liszt with recent publications of the nationalist composers. For many years there circulated a happy legend, based on a letter that has since been exposed as a fake, that during this 1873 visit to Liszt, Bessel brought with him a freshly minted copy of *The Nursery* (its cover designed by Ilya Repin) and left it with the virtuoso pianist. Liszt, so the story goes, picked up Musorgsky's song cycle during a dinner party and, carrying it casually to the keyboard, played it through with mounting excitement. He immediately wrote its author an impassioned letter with his reactions.[10] (Needless to say, Musorgsky never received this letter.)

What really happened was less dramatic, but still promising. Liszt did receive *The Nursery*, albeit only by post and some weeks later; he liked it so much that he wished to dedicate "*une bluette*" to its author. Upon hearing this news in St. Petersburg from Bessel's brother, Musorgsky was thrilled. In July 1873 he wrote a lengthy and ecstatic letter to Stasov, who at the time was vacationing with his family in Vienna, declaiming how much he deplored his clerking in the Forestry department, how hotly *Khovanshchina* was "boiling," how much "we need Europe, but not just to ride around on it, it's necessary to examine it," and he then asked Stasov wistfully: "Will you see Liszt, *généralissime?*" (L, 227). But it was not until Stasov called on Liszt and wrote urgent pleas to Musorgsky to join them that the nature of the temptation and the composer's resistance to it became clear.

Glimpses of Musorgsky in 1873 do not easily cohere into a single picture. In his letters he exults in his work on the new opera, which is "ripening" within him; he is also deeply moved by reports of Liszt's interest. "Stupid or not in music I may be," he wrote to Stasov in that same July letter,

> but in *The Nursery* it seems I was not stupid. Because an understanding for children and a view of them in their own little world, and not as amusing dolls, does not suggest a composer who is viewing things stupidly. All this may be so; but I never thought that Liszt – who, with very few exceptions, does colossal subjects – could grasp and appreciate *The Nursery* in a serious way and be deeply moved by it; why, all the children in it are so thoroughly Russian, with a powerful local smell ... when it becomes possible, I will skate off to him in Europe and entertain him with novelties ...

There were counter-signals, however, that his close friends could not fail to see. That July, Dmitry Stasov's wife Poliksena wrote to Musorgsky from Salzburg: "Nice, dear Musoryanin, what's this I hear? My husband writes me that he has found you looking thinner, quite changed ... in general not Musoryanin-like ... what depresses you? The office work? Let them pass you by with their promotions, don't waste yourself ... Is it possible you will ruin yourself prematurely, as Glinka ruined himself? ..." (L, 222). In reply, Musorgsky wrote an elaborate, affectionate, but evasive letter. To the Stasovs' sister Nadezhda in St. Petersburg he adopted a jocular tone: "*Khovanshchina* is boiling, but it's too soon to commit it to paper. I've become so severe with myself that it's laughable, and the more severe I become, the more disorderly I behave . . . Severe to myself and still disorderly, [signed] Musoryanin" (L, 237). Early in August, from Vienna, Stasov telegraphed Musorgsky a concrete invitation to visit Liszt together. Musorgsky wired back a single word: "Impossible."

Stasov would not accept this refusal. Surely you could take one week's leave from work, he reasoned in his next letter, even if your chief is sick ("he won't be sick forever"); perhaps you can even quit that department and look for a post elsewhere; because "for us to lose Liszt – this would be an unpardonable sin: naturally I won't go to him alone, but together – God knows when we would have another chance" (L, 241–46). Of course Stasov could not go alone, because he was only the harbinger and publicist of creative genius, not genius itself. Only the delivery of his protégé in person would constitute the intimate service he craved to perform for Liszt. Stasov traveled to Paris and continued to wait. But then Musorgsky's alibi shifted. "I forced myself to answer immediately your powerful call to *Europe* – to *Liszt*," he wrote to Stasov at the beginning of September (L, 247). "But at the same time I forced myself to realize that *Khovanshchina* had to be started, because its time had come . . . Reading these lines, you are thinking: that rascal Musoryanin, why does he remain silent about Liszt? IMPOSSIBLE. Don't curse me . . ."

Musorgsky's reluctance to show himself during that summer of 1873 was a pivotal event. Waiting on the fate of *Boris* must have increased his anxiety; being between homes and housemates did not help. To this destabilized environment one must add the unexpected death, at the end of July, of Viktor Hartmann, artist, architect, and Musorgsky's close friend. As we saw in the case of his mother's death eight years earlier, such losses were poorly borne by Musorgsky and often triggered bouts of his "nervous illness." And yet there is a mocking resilience – both pathetic and perverse – in Musorgsky's correspondence during these months. Only partly in jest, he requests

Stasov *not* to refrain from reminding him that he let Liszt slip; as he wrote his mentor in early August, at times "a loathsome feeling and sense of aversion" is good, it "rouses the brains," and "for a Russian this is always useful, because a Russian (whoever he may be) can be compared with a St. Petersburg cabdriver, who with particular gusto dozes off at the very moment he's carrying a customer" (L, 239). Could Musorgsky have been so indispensable at his clerking job, which he loathed, that he could not have taken a week's leave? Money was not the issue (he thanked Stasov for "guaranteeing the financial side" of the journey); and the excuse that *Khovanshchina*'s "time had come" was hard to sustain, since, for all the excitement, only two brief episodes from Act 3 were actually written down during those months. Later, Stasov suggested that Musorgsky could not trust Liszt's sympathy and was surprised and intimidated by it. A more likely explanation is that Musorgsky could not trust himself.

Borodin and Rimsky-Korsakov provide the most distressed hypotheses about this summer. "Here is pitiful and sorrowful news about the author of *Boris*," Borodin wrote to his wife at the end of October. "He has been drinking heavily. Nearly every day he sits in the Maly Yaroslavets restaurant on Morskaya Street, often drinking himself stiff. This summer the Sorokins saw him completely drunk in Pavlovsk; he caused a disturbance there; the affair reached the police . . . This is horribly sad! Such a talented man sinking so low morally. Now he periodically disappears . . ." (L, 252). Rimsky-Korsakov draws a similar portrait in his memoirs. "A certain mysteriousness, a haughtiness, appeared in him," Rimsky wrote of Musorgsky in the mid-1870s. "His self-conceit grew enormously. It was often impossible to understand his stories, conversations, and those sallies which he intended as wit." Although Musorgsky would refuse wine when offered it with respectable friends, every night he was drawn to Maly Yaroslavets, where, as Rimsky records it, the drinkers in this new circle of boon companions would "out-cognac themselves" [*prokon'iachit'sia*]. "Flashes of powerful creativeness continued in him for a long time," Rimsky acknowledged, "but his mental logic was growing dim, slowly and gradually."[11]

In the fall of 1874, Musorgsky took joint lodgings with Count Arseny Golenishchev-Kutuzov, an aspiring young poet, playwright, aesthete, and distant relative. In his memoirs of the composer (which, as the Epilogue shall attest, enter into posthumous competition with Stasov for control of Musorgsky's biography), the Count does not mention his housemate's alcoholism. But he readily mentions those other aspects of Musorgsky's personality that the *kuchkist* colleagues noted with such growing despair. "It was fate that brought Musorgsky and me together," Golenishchev-Kutuzov notes with disarming candor (MR, 84). "Both of us were deeply convinced of our genius and decided that, without fail, each of us would say a 'new word' in his own field. Musorgsky was older than I; he already belonged to a 'circle'; he had his admirers, people who valued him; and worst of all, he had his mentors. He believed that the 'new word in music' had already been spoken by him. What he still needed to do was to make that 'word' universal property. But I was still very timid . . ."

The rapid and deep friendship that the composer developed with Golenishchev-Kutuzov at this time explains a great deal. Musorgsky was tired of being "sponsored" by others and wished to be a mentor to someone younger and more impressionable. Optimally, this would be a person desirous of serving his *own* goals and the cause of art, not the general (and fickle) public. In his biography of the composer, Dobrovensky strikes the proper chord. "The new friendship was an essential counterweight," he writes.

> Where Stasov's interests ended, there Golenishchev-Kutuzov
> pricked up his ears. A lover of "absolute beauty," Arseny Arkadievich
> could not remake the composer after his own fashion. But he could
> support those sides of Musorgsky's talent that were of no interest to
> Vladimir Stasov. What is more, the young poet's tendency to
> reflection, to mournful musings, corresponded somewhat to the
> change that was coming upon Musorgsky himself by slow degrees,
> and that was gradually growing denser in the very air of the epoch.[12]

For a time, Musorgsky tried to promote his new friend to Stasov, whose support the composer never ceased to need. "Since Pushkin and Lermontov I have not encountered what I find in Kutuzov," Musorgsky wrote to Stasov in June 1873, with bewildering overstatement.

> This is no manufactured poet, like Nekrasov [a civic poet of the sixties, known for his poetry on behalf of oppressed classes]... For our young poet (and he is *very young*) has not been carried away by the civic motif, that is, he hasn't remade himself according to fashion and he hasn't gone aping Nekrasov, like some monkey... This *aristocracy of the brains*, above all, is what has comforted me... Kutuzov is a *good judge of himself* (Balakirev used to say, an "inner critic"), as every genuine artist must be... And one further observation: a poet can be fully sincere only with those things which he has known *closely*: thus Kutuzov hasn't done one social motif, not a single Nekrasovian grief. (L, 217–18)

Musorgsky ended this letter (which was remarkably naive, given Stasov's radical-left politics) by angling for an invitation. "Let me bring Kutuzov over tomorrow; if you approve of him, you will accept him as you have me." We do not know Stasov's reaction to this bald prompt. But shining through Musorgsky's defense of the young poet is a reconfirmation of his own personal faith. He had spoken a "new word" and he stands by it. Without ceasing to hope for the world's acceptance of this word, and with all the severe handicaps imposed by a growing chemical addiction, Musorgsky would now submit only to his own aesthetic judgment and create "sincerely," out of what he knew.

"None of us knew the real subject and plan of *Khovanshchina*," Rimsky recalled of the mid-1870s. "From Musorgsky's accounts – flowery, affected, and overly intricate (for such was his style of expression then), it was hard to grasp its subject as something whole and consecutive."[13] From 1872 to 1880, Musorgsky worked fitfully on this second historical opera. At his death it was still incomplete, and only in piano-vocal score. It is an amazing construct, with a sense of wholeness and consequence quite outside what Rimsky or Stasov were prepared to acknowledge. Underlying the opera is a vision of history, transcendence, and love that significantly departs from the expression of those values in Boris Godunov. It also departs significantly from the other historical operas of its time.

"It was I who suggested the subject to him, in the spring of 1872, even before Boris had been staged in the theatre," Stasov wrote of Khovanshchina, adding blandly: "It seemed to me that the struggle between old and new Russia, the passing from the scene of the first and the birth of the second, would be rich soil for drama and opera, and Musorgsky shared my opinion."[14] Like Rimsky-Korsakov, Stasov became gradually and irreversibly disillusioned with Musorgsky's handling of the project. "Musorgsky devoted himself to the opera with great enthusiasm, and his research on the sources – dissenters' texts, Old Russian texts, the seventeenth century in general – was enormous," Stasov recalled.

> His numerous and often verbose letters to me from this epoch are full of details of his research . . . The very best of what he composed, at times showing signs of splendid and enormous talent, belongs to the period 1872–75. After that, under the influence of weakening health and a shattered organism, his talent began to weaken and, it appears, to change. His compositions became foggier, more fussily mannered, sometimes even incoherent and tasteless. In order to finish the opera more quickly, as it was becoming beyond his strength, he thoroughly remade the libretto and threw out many scenes, details, persons – often, it must be said, to the opera's detriment.

As usual, Stasov was partly correct. He did provide the theme. But then he meddled mightily in Musorgsky's realization of it, and at a time when the composer could not afford to lose friends. It was hardly surprising that the "struggle between old and new Russia" had "occurred to Stasov" in 1872, for almost nothing else was in the air. In May of that year, the bicentennial of Peter the Great's birth was launched in the imperial capital. This jubilee affirmed Russia's modernization and material progress, culminating a process that had begun in 1812 with the expulsion of Napoleon. Russia, at last, had

14   Poster for 1897 St. Petersburg production of
     Khovanshchina, in Rimsky-Korsakov's edition, by
     the Russian Private Opera

caught up with Western Europe. Finally, the violent abruptness of Peter's reforms was justified – and their progressive vision confirmed – by the current reigning, reformist emperor, Alexander II. Although nothing like the euphoria of the early 1860s (the government's erratic, capricious, and backsliding policies since the Great Reforms had seen to that), an optimism about history seized the intelligentsia, left and right.

Two weeks into this noisy celebration, Musorgsky wrote to Stasov the first of his ecstatic letters about his future *Khovanshchina*. In it, he displays a type of patriotism that the jubilee celebrants would have found most uncongenial. Populist and retrograde at the same time, even pagan with its subtext of primitive Eros and despair, Musorgsky's imagery suggests a radically different sense of the workings of time. "What if Musoryanin were to thunder over Mother Russia!" he wrote to Stasov (L, 185–86).

> More than once have I plowed the black earth, and I want to plow the unfertilized, virgin earth; not merely to be acquainted with the people, but I thirst to be their brother; it's frightening, but good! . . . The power of the black earth will make itself manifest, when you plow to the very bottom. It is possible to plow the black earth with tools wrought of alien materials. And at the end of the seventeenth century they did plow Mother Russia with such tools, and she could not immediately discern with what they were plowing, and how the black earth *opened up* and began to *breathe*. And there the beloved Mother gave herself to sundry actual and privy councillors and they gave her, the long-suffering one, no time to collect herself . . . "*Where're we headed?*" [Russia asked]. The ignorant and the confused were put to death: *force!* . . . "We've gone forward," – you lie. "*We haven't moved!*" Paper, books, they've gone forward – but we haven't moved . . . Public benefactors will seek to glorify themselves and shore up their glory in documents, but the people groan, and to stifle their groans they drink like the devil, and groan worse than ever: *haven't moved!*

Against the dynamic affirmations of the Petrine jubilee, Musorgsky posits, in this strangely incantational letter, a passionate stubborn heaviness. Such immobility, with its intoxication and almost Oblomov-like resistance to the bullying enticements of progress, was to remain at the center of Khovanshchina. Stasov did not hide his displeasure. Very soon their opinions on the shape of the project diverged. Musorgsky tried hard, and unsuccessfully, to win over his mentor. For it became increasingly clear that "the passing from the scene of old Russia and the birth of the new" was, in Musorgsky's view, no straightforward historical process that would guarantee a jubilee after two centuries had passed. It was a rich and spiritually complex event, with tragedy in some realms and triumph in others. In the opera, the tragedy and the triumph are distributed in a wholly unprecedented way.

For those with ears to hear, the plot of the opera had quite a contemporary resonance. Delusionary efforts at reform collide with utopian dreams and a recalcitrant populace – and spark violence. Most of the action in Khovanshchina takes place in Moscow, 1682. The future Peter the Great is only ten years old, co-reigning with his feeble stepbrother. The city is at the mercy of rowdy bands of musketeers under the protection of the boyar Ivan Khovansky. The regent Sophia, Peter's halfsister, is introducing Western reforms under her chief minister and former lover, Prince Golitsyn. Opposed to those reforms – to all reforms – are the so-called "Old" (or as they preferred, the "True") Believers, a militant group of religious dissenters that saw the hand of the Antichrist in all modernization and preferred mass suicide to submission to the contaminated state. In the 1680s, Sophia's search-and-destroy missions against Old Believer communities resulted in an epidemic of immolations. The opera's final act realistically commemorates just such a scene: convinced of the end of the world, the spiritual leader Dosifei (modeled on the great martyr the Archpriest Avvakum, b. 1620, burned at the stake, 1682) eventually leads his faithful into an oiled hermitage, which is then put to the torch.

That is the finale, the "passing of old Russia from the scene." But in the preceding acts, the "birth of new Russia" is scarcely presented in a more hopeful vein. Musorgsky compressed a number of later events into one ghoulish string of banishments and deaths. Ivan Khovansky is murdered at his estate, among his dancing girls and concubines, by order of Tsar Peter. Prince Golitsyn is stripped of his power and exiled. Andrei Khovansky, Ivan's philandering and frivolous son, runs for protection to his former mistress Marfa, an Old Believer, and is ushered together with her into the burning hermitage. For the dissenters' chants, Musorgsky consulted priests, sextons, folklorists. "I am gathering such folk-honey from all quarters," he wrote Stasov in July 1873, "to make the honeycomb tastier and *more like itself*, because, after all, this is a people's drama" (L, 226).

In Russian, the phrase *narodnaya drama* ("people's drama") is polyvalent: it can mean popular drama, national drama, or a drama of the folk [*narod*]. For Stasov, it meant one thing: a drama that invests all virtue, importance, passion, and compassion in the common people. In a letter from Vienna (the one in which he refused to accept his friend's verdict of "impossible" regarding the hoped-for visit to Liszt), Stasov vigorously resisted Musorgsky's intent to be faithful to historical fact and thus give major roles in the opera (as it happened, spiritually elevated roles) to the high-born. Regardless of their historical prototypes, the carriers of all true morality in the opera – the Old Believers Dosifei and Marfa – must not be "aristocrats who have laid aside their rank," Stasov wrote, but "real people of the soil." Redo the operatic plan, Stasov recommended in a letter from August 1873, so that women of the lower orders stand out against the corruption of the upper classes and "a new side of ancient Russia is portrayed: petty, wretched, dull-brained, envious, evil, and malicious" (L, 244). Three years later, Stasov's advice to his friend was still the same. "Too little activity of individual personalities," he wrote in mid-May 1876, "too many 'purposeless' quarrels" between factions (L, 333–34). Perhaps the soothsayer Marfa could become Golitsyn's mistress, he suggested. Give the audience genuine interactions; add some passion to the opera's present.

Stasov's advice was not entirely bad, and Musorgsky did incorporate some of it. But he refused to simplify the class origins of the pro-

15 Sofia Petrovna Preobrazhenskaya (1904–1966), in the
role of the Old Believer Marfa in *Khovanshchina*

tagonists in a "populist" direction. Also, he would not transform Marfa, for all her smoldering love and passionate memory, into an ordinary jealous opera diva. She remains dark, detached, stern, unconsummated; here again we sense Musorgsky's subliminal revisionist view of sexuality, closer to the pagan concept of the goddess Mother Moist Earth than to any possessable female image. He also resolutely rejected any suggestion on Stasov's part that the "new" *wins out* over the "old." The black earth was plowed, agitated, confused, in fertile gestation – but basically its inhabitants hadn't moved.

Since *Khovanshchina*, unlike recent revivals of *Boris Godunov*, is known almost solely in Rimsky-Korsakov's redaction, one textological comment is in order. Among the most stirring effects of its final scene are Peter's trumpets, resounding offstage in a brilliant Preobrazhensky march while the hermitage goes up in flames. This vigorous music (heralding the "new world," the forward march of history) is opposed to the Old Believer hymn (thin, mystical, backward-looking) that the shrouded dissenters sing as they mount their funeral pyre. It is important to know that these trumpets – and a great deal else in the final act, both in the music and the words – are wholly Rimsky-Korsakov's invention. The stageworthiness of this ending strategy is beyond dispute, and there is even some sentimental justification for it: the Preobrazhensky Guards were the regiment of both Peter the Great and Modest Musorgsky. What is more, *Khovanshchina*'s finale had only been sketched out: who knows exactly what Musorgsky would have done? By censor regulations, of course, he could not have brought Tsar Peter, a Romanov, on stage even had he wished to. But there is evidence that Musorgsky came to feel the opera was stronger for leaving Peter altogether in the wings.[15] By adding the trumpeters' march in his completion of his friend's unfinished work, Rimsky made up for the absence of a tsar on stage as far as was legally possible. It profoundly altered the historical worldview of the opera.

More, even, than *Boris Godunov*, Musorgsky's second historical opera must be "de-Rimskified" if its author's sense of historical truth is to be glimpsed. Musorgsky began one of his *Khovanshchina* letters to

Stasov in July 1872 with a musical example and quote from the ending of his first opera: "'Soon the foe will come and darkness will set in. Impenetrable darkness' – thus whines the holy fool in my *Boris*, and, I'm afraid, not in vain" (L, 188–89). The ending scene of *Boris* represented the negating, nihilistic pole of Russian historical experience. After 1605 came the Time of Troubles, and then the slow consolidation of power by the early Romanovs. The first deep crisis of the new dynasty, the non-cooperation of the breakaway Old Believers in the 1680s, was this darkness returned. Again it seemed as if the Russian state might come to its end. Again Musorgsky had chosen to dramatize an epoch in which no wholeness, no shared national worldview, could be found.

But how does one set up a dramatic or musical "conversation" between radically incompatible worldviews? It is significant that Musorgsky composed *Khovanshchina* without a ready libretto. Even more remarkably, it had no single identifiable literary source. Like the Kromy Forest finale in *Boris*, Musorgsky intuited the truth of an entire *scene* and then sought (in archival publications and history books) the words, documents, interactions, conversations, and harmonic and melodic contours to fill it out. In this task, his apprenticeship with Gogol's *Marriage* had given him great dexterity. But that had been speech-setting at close quarters – as he put it in 1877, an "étude for a chamber trial"[16] – and part of Musorgsky's "new word" for the grander, more fully dramatic stage was to enlarge the domain over which an intoned utterance might have sway. His practice with the humbler genres prepared him for this more ambitious undertaking.

Musorgsky had learned that talk between people is not just what one hears on the surface. It is fraught, dreamy, doublevoiced, partly in denial and full of missed cues. Often an inner or submerged intonation is picked up by one party and becomes the dominant theme in the exchange. (Dostoevsky was a great master at these multi-layered, psychologically intricate dialogues.) What is more, as in "Svetik Savishna," even conversation based on real-life events in naturalistic settings can be highly stylized: an accurate presentation of the village idiot's "real psychological life" was precisely this wedding song projected in fantasy within a wretchedly prosaic situation. Thus stylization itself enters the conversation, tunes it up, mediates the world we live in and the world we yearn for. As Musorgsky well knew, this mediation, along with the ordered emotional release it made possible, was the primary social function of folk formulas set to music.

But neither the crude topical conversation of Gogol's comic play, nor the folk-lament-cum-wedding-song of the village idiot, had any historical dimension. A broad historical canvas required other more visionary skills. Musorgsky, it seems, was drawn to moments of crisis – points at which dynasties, worldviews, and whole languages come into conflict and are forced to change – precisely as grist to test the elasticity of dialogue. In *Boris Godunov*, the task was easier because approached through Pushkin's play, a work of Shakespearean proportions compressed into austere, sparse pentameters by Russia's greatest poet. No such prism existed for the historical texture of *Khovanshchina*. Curiously, although set in a more recent time, the second opera sounds much older. Following his practice in the Kromy scene of *Boris*, Musorgsky drew on unpoeticized texts for his libretto; many of them are raw seventeenth-century documents.

What is more, *Khovanshchina* has no title hero. It has a pair of troublemakers, the Khovanskys father and son (the -*shchina* suffix in Russia here signifies "the mess stirred up" by the preceding proper noun); and it has a series of powerful antagonistic groups, each with its own leader. What governs the behavior of these groups is not the usual conflict governing historical drama, namely, patriotism versus love; that was the *Salammbô* plot, and Musorgsky quickly tired of it. In *Khovanshchina*, more archaic obsessions are at work. There is the fixed system of genealogical rank so sacred to old Muscovy (and infinitely more central to its sense of dignity than the more operatic modes of Western chivalry or romance). There is the arrival of the Antichrist in the person of Tsar Peter, following hard upon the apocalyptic Year of the Beast, 1666. And overarching all is the quest for True Russia, essentially *a*historical. For these reasons, Musorgsky refused to follow the time-honored convention for ending historical opera, in which a resolution of the plot on the erotic plane – that is, consummation of love between a hero and a heroine – is allowed to resolve problems on the historical plane. Russian history, he believed, was not that easily managed. Thus at almost all points where opera plots usually cohere, this one falls apart. No wonder Rimsky-Korsakov found it difficult to "grasp its subject as something whole and consecutive." As in Russian Orthodox icons, where each living body commands its own perspective and requires the observer to enter its realm and look out through its eye, each group in *Khovanshchina* is whole unto itself and follows its own truth.

This dynamic governs much of the logic of the opera. "Stylized" musical components (tuneful leitmotifs for the heroes and heroines, religious chants, dirges, dances, folk melodies), self-righteous proclamations, and autonomous worldviews are everywhere juxtaposed – although a common language among them, such as might enable genuine "listening acts," fails to coalesce. A conversation between musical genres and social classes is conducted that is unresolvable by any of the actors on stage. Only some "new word" can resolve the crisis, but this word is spoken in a realm unavailable to characters and audience alike. This is the realm of the Old (True) Believers, who time and again emphasize that they are not *in* Russia but are seeking her.

When in the final act the True Believers depart into what looks to outsiders like death, they leave the sinful sublunary realm far behind. For this reason alone, Rimsky-Korsakov's trumpets are misleading. If heard at all, they must be heard as heavenly trumpets, not as a feeble attempt to set up an earthly kingdom to last a thousand years. By the end, every "politician" is either exiled or dead. Tsar Peter is nowhere to be seen, and all worthy people in the opera are already impervious to his threat. In a letter to Stasov of August 1873, Musorgsky described the princes' quarrel in Act 2. His intent, he wrote, was to "reveal this loathsome conference at Golitsyn's in its true light, where they're all grabbing at the throne and scepter, and probably Dosifei is the only one with a firmly fixed conviction" (*L*,

16 Kurilko's stage design for Act 4 of Khovanshchina

240). The conviction firmly fixed in Dosifei is that the new order is fated to perish in the face of the old – and that the old will last forever.

This interpretation – in which history moves backward, not forward – would explain other symmetries in the opera's plot structure, as well as its glorious simplification at the end. Musorgsky spent some time tracking down the proper Old Believer hymns, which, as he wrote one informant, would be given "in unison" at the end of the opera (L, 277). The end could only be realized in unity, as the outcome of a cosmic confrontation. The two major realms in *Khovanshchina* are history and faith. Scenes in the opera end either on a denunciation (the signature motif of the history plot) or on prayer – which connotes fidelity, renunciation, submission to fate, and love. History in the opera is one uninterrupted tissue of violence, lies, political ambition, and murder. Only prayer is large enough to confront and defeat this reality of "death-in-history." And in fact, faith turns out to be far more complex, difficult, and toughminded than anything the politicians have to offer. It is neither aggressive nor ascetic (Marfa remains passionately in love with Andrei Khovansky, despite his betrayal), but it puts absolutely no trust in the workings of time in this world. When Marfa asks Dosifei to kill her on the spot if her love for Prince Andrei is sinful, the majestic old man replies: "In God's will is our unfreedom. Love as you have always loved, and all that you have suffered will itself pass." There is no recrimination or denial, no passing of judgment, no sanction to separate the realms of body and spirit. It is a specifically Russian transcendence. Wait, continue to love, and history itself (at least the sort of history that produces empires and broken hearts) will come to an end. If *Boris* concludes in negation and darkness, then the end of *Khovanshchina* is a utopia of the liberated spirit.

In his final years, the composer found it increasingly difficult to transcribe the opera he had innerly composed. Stasov continued to send his correctives; Musorgsky would fall silent. "*Khovanshchina* is too big, too extraordinary a task," he wrote to Stasov in June 1876, after receiving one such piece of advice (L, 338). "I have halted work – I have fallen into thought." Stasov nudged him round with a mix of

17   Musorgsky seated at the piano, 1873

carrot and stick. "Let's hold off your starting lessons in polyphony with Rimsky, and meanwhile, how like a lion you move ahead!" Stasov wrote back caressingly in August of that year (L, 344). "There is every-thing in abundance in your opera so far . . . Only one thing is lacking: an active political element, *undertaking* something, *aimed at some purpose.*" Stasov was more correct about this lack than he wished to acknowledge. It could be argued that the absence of such politicking purpose (with its concomitant shrill belief in progress) was one of the opera's most potent articles of faith.

Long after Musorgsky's death, Igor Stravinsky arranged the aston-ishing final scene of *Khovanshchina* in a trumpetless redaction for Diaghilev's Paris premiere of the opera on the eve of the First War. Gone were Rimsky's thrilling bugles announcing Peter the Great; all that was heard at the final curtain were those two hymns accompany-ing the Old Believers to their glory. This scene was performed in 1913 and then withheld from repertory until 1986. To grasp properly Musorgsky's sense of history, one must hear the final scene in this way, as the composer left it, "from the inside." The only means we have to conquer death is to create an autonomous worldview, or a musical world, that has moved beyond it.

5 The 1870s: Musorgsky and death

In July 1873, a difficult and lonely summer, Musorgsky wrote to Dmitry Stasov's wife Poliksena in Germany:

> Vityushka Hartmann died in Moscow of an aneurysm. Such grief! O long-suffering Russian art! . . . What might Hartmann have gone on to do! . . . Beautiful sounds are always beautiful and they so captivate a Little-Russian at a dumpling feast that he gobbles up those dumplings, he is drenched in melted butter and tears and he gulps down both the dumplings and the beautiful sounds. But something more substantial is needed. Art must embody not only beauty. A building is good when, in addition to a beautiful façade, it is well-planned and solid, when one can sense the aim of the construction and the whole head of the artist is visible. All this was in the perished Hartmann. (L, 230)

The passage abounds in Musorgsky's signature motifs. Musical beauty alone is static and even cowardly; it stupefies us, like overeating. Art requires intellectual discipline, visual and spatial concreteness. And the artist's "whole head," both the idiosyncratic face and the brains at work behind it, must be invested in the product. Musorgsky had befriended Viktor Hartmann (1834–73) in 1870. A genre-painter, designer, illustrator, and architect, Hartmann was one of several visual artists who served the composer as a model for creative imagination. Gradually, Musorgsky was replacing the musical circles that had dominated his life during the previous decade with historians, folklorists, painters. Although these men were all curious about the Russian folk and the forms of its art, not all were the civic-activist type of populist (Hartmann himself, with his leisurely travels and sketching tours through Europe, was certainly not).[1] His death was the first loss Musorgsky suffered from this new, extra-musical circle of friends.

Death, too, was appallingly concrete. Musorgsky developed several dramatic and musical means for dealing with it. One solution was encountered in *Khovanshchina*: create a population on stage that does not believe in death "down below" – and then turn over the final scene of the opera entirely to that group, at its moment of glory, removing all other possible perspectives. (It is no accident that the most elaborate and enthusiastic comments to Stasov concern this final mass leave-taking, full of white shrouds and green candles.) Musorgsky's fascination with death in that opera is not so much necrophiliac as transfigurative. Dying is an outlet, obligating all who witness it to new expression. Such also was the case with Viktor Hartmann. The piano suite *Pictures from an Exhibition*, devoted to Hartmann's memory and to his drawings, is a work of great visual and rhythmic power at several creative, and re-creative, levels. It is constructed so that we "see" the content of the pictures, "see" and "hear" the composer of *Pictures* as he walks from picture to picture in the gallery, even hear and see the musician-virtuoso creating music at the keyboard. All mortal parties in these scenarios are commemorated and preserved – and remarkably, musical tones alone are sufficient for their realization.

A final strategy for dealing with death was employed by Musorgsky in his last monumental treatment of the theme: the vocal cycle *Songs and Dances of Death* (1875–77). In that cycle, poetry and music combine to create a picture not of death in the abstract – timeless, shapeless, inert – but of dying as a process. Death itself is shown to be immortal. It possesses a body, an energy; it "arrives" on the scene to negotiate and beckon. Unlike the realm into which the Old Believers pass at the end of *Khovanshchina*, Death in the vocal cycle is a personality with a voice. Is this death or eternal life? In the mid-1870s, Musorgsky was much taken up with that question and its musical resolution. To grasp its apotheosis in these great works on death, we must back up and consider Musorgsky's visual and dramatic imagination.

In July 1872, the composer wrote to Stasov in a confessional but belligerent tone on the matter of music and the other arts.

> Why, *tell me*, when I listen to the conversation of young artists – painters or sculptors . . . – I can follow their turns of thought, their ideas, their aims, and seldom do I hear anything said about technique – unless it's necessary. And why, *do not tell me*, when I listen to our musical brethren, do I so seldom hear a vital idea, but mostly stuff from a school-room bench – technique and musical ABC's? . . . Maybe I'm afraid of technique because I'm poor at it. However, there are some who will stand up for me in art and in this respect also. (L, 191–93)

Musorgsky suggests here that reducing art to mere "technique" debases conversation and too easily conceals a poverty of ideas. Such a reduction is also aesthetically inappropriate. Typically, he draws a culinary analogy: when we eat a tasty pot pie, do we really want to hear about events in the kitchen, the cook's filthy apron, "a million *poods* of butter, five hundred eggs, a gutted fish, some intestines peeping out of a sieve . . . In ripe artistic productions there is an aspect of chaste purity, that when touched by dirty paws, grows loathsome." A finished artwork *lives*; its component parts – before the artist touches them – are dead. Why, he goes on to ask, do Ilya Repin's canvases "Barge-haulers on the Volga" or "Village Religious Procession" *live*, and live to such an extent that, upon viewing them and getting to know them, we say of them: "you are the very ones I wanted to see"? Why, he asks, is our recent music not alive in that way?

The position Musorgsky advocates here – music on behalf of the living image – is an ancient dream of the temporal arts, and ludicrously easy to caricature. *Kuchkist* composers (and none more often than Musorgsky) were routinely accused of replacing real, that is, autonomous, music with everyday "scenes" and naturalistic "sounds." Even dissidents on the literary left, whose sympathy might have been expected, joined the chorus of debunkers. In 1874, in a wicked lampoon, the great satirist Saltykov-Shchedrin described a drunken "Vasily Ivanych" [Musorgsky] dozing and wheezing on a couch, attended by a spin doctor [Stasov] convinced that every wheeze is "another idea!" and who rushes to record from the mouth of the musician every "moo" ("Vasily Ivanych always expresses his feelings in simple sounds").[2] More serious were the reviews that pretended to musical judgment. Commenting in 1872 on a rumored performance of Musorgsky's *Marriage* at an opera singer's benefit concert (the rumor was unfounded), one anonymous writer for the *Stock Exchange News* observed that "realism in music, painting with sounds, has been carried to such an extreme that it is impossible to go any further. With his *Marriage*, Mr. Musorgsky is saying 'whoa!' to opera – and it comes to a halt forever . . ." In fact, the columnist continues, "experts" have concurred that the best moment in *Marriage* is where "Podkolyosin and his fiancée pass the time in pleasant silence; of course the singers are silent, the orchestra is silent, and the audience is silent, stupefied by the sublimity of the music in the preceding scenes. They say that this moment in the opera is the peak of perfection and musical truth, before which pales the celebrated pause following the murder of the Commendatore in Mozart's *Don Giovanni*."[3]

Amid all this banal lampooning, of course, the only opponents worthy of serious attention were other composers of genius. In January 1878, Tchaikovsky wrote from San Remo to Madame von Meck:

> You are quite correct in characterizing Musorgsky as hopeless. His talent is perhaps the most remarkable of these [nationalist composers]. But he has a narrow nature . . . and a low nature, one which loves all that is coarse, crude, rough . . . He coquettes with his illiteracy and takes pride in his ignorance . . . But he has a real, even an original talent . . . A Musorgsky, for all his ugliness, speaks a new language. Beautiful it may not be, but it is fresh. (L, 366)

Coarse, crude, ugly, palpable, *fresh*: Musorgsky himself would not have disdained this part of Tchaikovsky's verdict. The "Mighty

18 The Makovskys' caricature of Stasov and the "Mighty Little Heap" "Procession into the Temple of Glory," 1871

Handful" almost begged to be drawn. It was a cartoonist's dream. In a famous caricature of 1871, "Procession into the Temple of Glory," Stasov is depicted as a peasant with bast sandals, horn, and drum, Balakirev as a bear, Hartmann as a monkey, the Purgold sisters as two trained lapdogs, Rimsky-Korsakov as a lobster, Cui as a fox with wreaths to distribute but with claws bared – and up front, crowing and prancing, Musorgsky leads this barnyard crew as a rooster.[4] If Romanticism had striven to elevate and, as it were, "aerate" physical images into music, then musical realism lowered sounds into pictures. On the surface, Musorgsky – backed up by the indefatigable Stasov – appears to have been the most radical practitioner of this ideology.

But whence, then, the lofty idealism that we sense so strongly in Musorgsky's comments about Hartmann (the "solid building" of his art), and what about Repin, whose canvases bring the dead to life? In a letter to Repin (who at the time was studying in Paris) from June 1873, Musorgsky wrote this paean to the visual arts (L, 215):

> Take your Volga barge-haulers (they are before me, I see them with my own eyes) – there's an ox and a goat and a sheep and a broken-down old mare and the devil knows how many other domestic animals, and here musicians get away with a variety of harmonies, and deal with technical peculiarities, and imagine that they are "creating types." It's sad. Long ago the artist-painter learned to mix his colors and work freely, if only God gave him a brain; but we musicians – first we think, then we measure off, then after measuring off, we think again – it's *childhood*, utter childhood – we're still infants!

For a "thinking musician," Musorgsky's visual appetite was voracious. Stasov, patron to realist painters and realist musicians alike, encouraged this trait in him. In the early 1870s, Stasov even put together a "troika" consisting of Musorgsky, Ilya Repin (1844–1930), and the sculptor Mark Antokolsky (1843–1902): three nationalist artists who created a Russia primarily out of what they *saw*. There were no verbal artists hitched to Stasov's cart. When in June 1873 Musorgsky recommended his new friend Golenishchev-Kutuzov for the post ("I dream" – he wrote to Stasov – "of a four-in-hand" [L, 218]), Stasov did not pick up on the idea. It appears that Stasov (like so many dogmatic realists, Leo Tolstoy among them) did not wholly trust words; he certainly did not trust poets. Words were ambiguous, images were not. Stasov, and the later socialist-realist critics who were his progeny, misunderstood the nature of Musorgsky's desire to interstitch the arts. Musorgsky was not opening up his musical world to perishable social and political influences, so that the indignities of the present could be fastened down and activists exhorted to resist them. That, for him, was not the purpose of the image in art. He was *capturing* that world and then transfiguring it from within, so that it would live forever.

When, a decade after Musorgsky's death, Repin was invited to participate in the restructuring of the Imperial Academy of Arts and in 1894 appointed a professor at that school, Stasov was outraged.[5] He denounced his former protégé – by then the most famous of the realist painters or "Itinerants"[6] – as a renegade, a "mercenary scoundrel" who had sold out to institutionalized art. Repin, who was born a crown serf, could not challenge the aristocratic Stasov to a duel; instead, he wrote him a dignified, mournful letter of farewell. He reminded his mentor that he had never forfeited the artist's right to paint free of extrinsic pressure, even back in the 1870s, and that reforming the Academy constituted its own sort of civic service. Stasov did not forgive the betrayal. By that time Ilya Repin had fame, a family, a secure European market for his paintings; he was not alone. Musorgsky in the 1870s had none of those things. Had the composer not been so grateful for Stasov's steady support and so very needful of friends, his own position might well have approximated Repin's. He would not have "fallen into thought" – that is, fallen silent – whenever an incompatible mandate arrived from Stasov on how to set *Khovanshchina* right. But the dependency was great, and to an extent it was mutual. In an appreciative note of October 1875 (after several humiliating months of arrears in his rent and apartment-hopping),

Musorgsky, gazing at a photograph that Stasov had sent of Repin's most recent portrait of him, played powerfully to the older man's needs. When Balakirev "held us in his iron grip" we were a "mighty heap," he wrote, but now "we have degenerated into cowardly trai-tors." Stasov exulted in such talk. "You wrote me just as Repin or Antokolya would have written," he shot back. "That's why you three are my trinity" (L, 311–13).

Musorgsky could hardly have resisted such an endorsement. But on matters of pure art and how to enable it, his confidant remained Golenishchev-Kutuzov. In September 1875, when the Count was laid up on his country estate with an injured leg, Musorgsky reported the latest news from the capital: Russia, having conquered Turkestan, was on the brink of war with Turkey. As Musorgsky wrote his friend:

> The eternal struggle of the Slavs with Islam, it's an old song. General madness while being penniless, general omniscience while being ignorant, trying to raise the level of the public masses by shouting for some sort of rights while the country hasn't a clue about rights; unconscious inertia . . . Let us speak of our modest world of art, let us lock ourselves in for a little while in a cozy corner and from there, close to life and to people but far from all these blathering tirades on rights, freedom, protest, let's look life boldly in the eye. This is necessary, because one must speak truth to people, not blather but genuine truth. (L, 307)

To "look life in the eye," an artist must transcend the topical. Only such transcendence held out promise of salvation. On this point, Musorgsky parted company with the more dogmatic of his "docu-menting" and "illustrating" friends among the visual artists – even though their passion for scientific concreteness often paralleled his own. Merely to *copy* life or to fix life in place was never Musorgsky's interest. Artistic activity must aim higher: it must rescue not only the artist (who was, by the nature of things, mortal) but *art itself* from oblivion. Instructive here is the scandal that surrounded "The Forgotten One" [*Zabytyi*], a painting by the celebrated war artist Vasily Vereshchagin (1844–1904).[7] Completed in 1871 after Vereshchagin's

19 Vereshchagin's canvas "The Forgotten One," from his Turkestan series, 1871

return from the Turkestan campaign, the canvas inspired a poetic ballad by Golenishchev-Kutuzov that Musorgsky then set to music in 1874. Although composer and artist did not meet until much later, each man in his own domain – Musorgsky in the realm of uttered sound, Vereshchagin in the sociology of war – had been deeply influenced by positivist historians and philosophers. Both believed that an accurate recording of human behavior must result in a "science" that would eventually yield laws, making possible the perfectability of the species. Vereshchagin was a soldier of immense courage. Decorated by the Russian military for bravery under fire (the grateful General Kaufman even offered to subsidize his canvases), he eventually perished at age sixty, while sketching aboard one of the Russian warships blown up by the Japanese near Port Arthur in 1904. As an artist, Vereshchagin specialized in death. The Turkestan series contained several unforgettable canvases, which caused a sensation among the artistic literati of Russia: a fatally wounded officer pitching forward with death in his eyes and mouth; a heap of blackened, shrunken Russian heads casually being toed by Muslim warriors as battle trophies; a pyramid of bones and skulls in the desert, called "The Apotheosis of War."

And then there was "The Forgotten One," the corpse of a soldier alone on a deserted Central Asian battlefield, his body being staked out by hungry vultures. With Stasov's help, Vereshchagin, already famous throughout Europe, mounted an exhibition of the Turkestan series in St. Petersburg in the spring of 1874. Musorgsky attended; so, too, did Emperor Alexander II, who was initially very enthusiastic about the show. The paintings were graphic proof of the barbarism of Russia's foes and the cost of civilization's forward march. But when he saw "The Forgotten One," he grimaced. "In my army such incidents cannot and could not happen," he remarked. When queried by the tsar's entourage, Vereshchagin admitted that he had not actually *seen* a dead soldier in such a pose, abandoned by his comrades and unburied. (What offended was not just the natural fact of death on a battlefield. In Russian folk culture, the earth is revered as clan mother;

thus an unburied body – a body not returned to Moist Mother Earth's nurturing bosom – is a special profanation. Its soul goes into limbo and becomes an orphan.) By imperial command, the Russian censor forbade any reproduction of "*Zabytyi*" in the Russian press for twenty years. That same evening, Vereshchagin suffered an attack of nerves and burned three of his paintings, including this offensive canvas.

Although photographs and studies of the painting did survive, it had been banished – and had perished. In autumn of that year, Golenishchev-Kutuzov wrote a poem (prudently called simply "Ballade," although subtitled "*Zabytyi*") describing ravens pecking at the unclosed eyes of a corpse while a young widow, back home in Russia, nurses an infant and dreams of her husband's return. Musorgsky provided the music. In December 1879, when Vereshchagin was leaving for Bulgaria to document the Russian army's pan-Slav adventure against the Turks, Stasov organized a reception for the departing artist. Musorgsky (who described the event in a letter to Kutuzov) was present. He performed the ballad at the piano for Vereshchagin; the artist was "touched to the soul," Musorgsky wrote, and in places even "taken over by nervous emotion" (L, 399). No music could bring back the dead soldier, of course, or consecrate him to the earth; art is not empowered to do that. But entropy had been reversed. The destroyed painting had been restored to life through this haunting ballad. And art, which is as immortal as both artist and artistic subjects are mortal, was confirmed.

Since one cannot literally resurrect the life of subjects, art itself – life's condenser – must be strenuously preserved from oblivion. Such was Musorgsky's task in *Pictures from an Exhibition*. Hartmann died at the end of July 1873. For Musorgsky, the next half-year was taken up with the triumph and furor of the *Boris Godunov* premiere, climaxing in January 1874. Two weeks later, a memorial exhibition of Hartmann's work (as many pieces as could be gathered together) opened in the Hall of the Academy of Artists in St. Petersburg, organized by Stasov and the president of the Architects' Society. It ran through March. When precisely Musorgsky visited the exhibit is unknown. We do know, thanks to the composer's careful dating, that the piano suite *Pictures from an Exhibition* was conceived and executed in twenty days, between the 2nd and the 22nd of June 1874. There is a brief note from Musorgsky to Stasov dated mid-June, with this progress report:

> Hartmann is boiling as Boris boiled. The sounds and the idea hung in the air, and now I am gulping and overeating. I can hardly manage to scribble it down on paper. I'm writing 4 numbers – with good transitions (on "promenade"). I want to do it as quickly and reliably as possible. My own physiognomy can be seen in the intermezzi. I consider it successful so far. I embrace you and take it that you are blessing me – so give me your blessing! (L, 271)

Eventually Musorgsky "illustrated" ten pictures in memory of Hartmann. He dedicated the composition to Stasov, who was thrilled with it – so much so that he could not resist claiming, much later, that he had a hand in selecting the topics. (On the envelope containing the composer's mid-June letter, Stasov noted affectionately: "Gartmanovshchina."[8]) Since four of the ten images by Hartmann that Musorgsky commemorated in *Pictures* are now lost, they survive only in verbal description and in this music. The situation recalls Vereshchagin's ill-starred canvas, "The Forgotten One." Indeed, without this tribute Hartmann himself very likely would have been forgotten. One month after completing the work, Musorgsky – who knew his own musical mind – wrote "for publication" on the title-page of the autograph. But, as one historian of *Pictures* has noted, "there is no evidence to suggest that any publisher was interested in the manuscript. He may well have fantasized about the success of his pieces and their appeal."[9] After Musorgsky's death, when Bessel & Co. acquired all rights (without fee) to the composer's unpublished works, Rimsky-Korsakov edited this work as well, but in a moderate, restrained way. *Pictures* appeared in print in 1886. It slumbered as a pianistic curiosity until Ravel's orchestration in 1922 – at which point all of its versions were restored to rapturous life.

A year after *Pictures from an Exhibition*, Musorgsky began another musical project with death at its center and pictorial drama as its

20   Viktor Hartmann (1842–1873), architect and artist, whose work inspired
Musorgsky's *Pictures from an Exhibition*

means. Its strategy was different, however, and the protagonists otherwise weighted. The vocal cycle *Songs and Dances of Death* (1875–77),
like the ballad "The Forgotten One," was a joint project with
Golenishchev-Kutuzov. It was Musorgsky's second large-scale col-
laboration with his housemate-poet. The first had taken place in 1874,
the cycle *Without Sun*, a setting of six lyrical poems about loneliness,
loss, the healing powers of nature, and the transitory relief offered by
memory. About this remarkable cycle of songs – which Debussy was
later to revere – Borodin wrote to his wife: "They all remind one of *Boris*
or else are the fruit of purely intellectual invention, and produce a very
unsatisfactory impression."[10] Stasov concurred. But Stasov was enormously excited by *Songs and Dances of Death*. It was he who encouraged
both poet and musician in this task and provided a number of the
scenarios.

Originally the cycle was very ambitious. Among Kutuzov's papers
(discovered only in 1935) was found a list of proposed entries: the
death of a rich man, a proletarian, a grand lady, a high official, the tsar,
a young girl, a peasant, a monk, a child, a merchant, a priest, a poet.
Musorgsky himself left piano sketches for a dying monk and for
a returning political exile who is shipwrecked and drowns within
sight of his native city. But out of this panorama of Russian deaths,
only four of Kutuzov's texts were eventually set to music (three in
1875, one in 1877) and arranged in a cycle. In June 1877, Dmitry Stasov
undertook to interest the Jurgenson music firm in the group. But – as
Musorgsky put it in a letter to Kutuzov in August of that year – having
"expressed *pleasure* in the proposition of publishing the Macabres, Mr.
Jurgenson then fell stubbornly silent" (L, 361). Apropos of the final
song "The Fieldmarshal" (where Death, mounted on horseback, sur-
veys a corpse-strewn battlefield), he added: "You can't possibly imagine, dear friend, the striking peculiarities of your picture when a
tenor sings it! Something nails you to the spot, you hear in it some
implacable, fatal love! Or to be more exact: this is death, coldly-
passionately in love with death, death taking its pleasure in death.
An unheard-of novel impression . . . Yes, after the war!"

21 Hans Holbein the Younger,
from the "Totentanz" cycle

At first the cycle was called simply "She" [Ona]. (In Russian, death [smert'] is a feminine noun.) This choice of title is significant. Widespread in Russian folk culture is a belief in naklikanie, the bringing-forth of something merely by speaking its name; to speak the name Death, therefore, is to invite her in, to summon her into existence. But in an unnerving logic, to posit only the pronoun in the title was to increase Death's power, for the entire cycle then unfolded under a dark feeling of taboo. Musorgsky was a creditable student of the occult, in both its European and its local Russian expression. He knew that in the Russian folk mind the act of naming was related not only to incarnation but also to the act of drawing pictures. (Repin had experienced this lesson the hard way, when he researched his "Bargehaulers on the Volga" during the summers of 1870 and 1871: the peasant haulers did not wish to pose, even for payment, because they held that once a person's image was transferred onto paper, his soul ceased to belong to him and could be sold to the devil.[11]) Musorgsky and Golenishchev-Kutuzov aimed to illustrate death, look it boldly in the eye and stare it down. Death could not, of course, be defeated – but, like all spirits in the quasi-pagan Russian countryside, it could be tricked, distracted, passed off on someone else. In composing the poem cycle and setting it to music, both poet and musician drew on Russian folk images as well as on a pan-European tradition.

In that larger tradition, the Grim Reaper was uncommonly severe. Fate was of more epic proportions, trickery less of an option. During the early 1870s, Musorgsky came to know Liszt's "Totentanz" and Saint-Saëns's "Danse macabre"; while the latter made a dismal impression (nothing, Musorgsky remarked, but a "sentimental miniature"), Liszt impressed him greatly, especially Death's dance elaborated as a set of variations on a "Dies irae." Kutuzov too was fascinated by the ambivalent medieval image of a seductive, dancing death. When he set about writing his poetic cycle, he selected four conventionally affirmative genres – lullaby, serenade, peasant dance, and triumphal march – and then made each of them grotesque and fatal by the unexpected entry of Death.

In the first poem, "Lullaby," Death steals into the room where a mother is tending her dying child, promising to provide better and more compassionate care for the suffering infant. In "Serenade," Death seduces a young girl who is dying of consumption, persuading her that unlike her earlier faithless suitors, he would be a true knight and tireless lover. In the third song, "Trepak" (the only one with a folk-loric base), Death in the guise of a blizzard freezes a poor drunken peasant on his way home from the tavern, bribing him out of his miserable life with a vision of an abundant harvest on a hot summer's day. In the final song, "The Fieldmarshal" (inspired by the slaughter along the fronts of the Russo-Turkish War in 1877), Death, a skeleton on horseback, appears after a battle to proclaim its victory over all adversaries and to pronounce its final judgment: that death is forever, that it has no meaning, and that there is no resurrection.

How did Musorgsky set these harrowing poems of Kutuzov's in keeping with his own song-writing aesthetic? Is there anything in common between these stylized encounters and the *Nursery* cycle he completed several years earlier? It would seem there is, although the method is applied to very different material. And here we glimpse the remarkably productive effect that poet and musician must have had on one another, in its own way as rich as the roommate relationship with Rimsky-Korsakov two years previously. Kutuzov was not only a lyric poet but also an aspiring playwright, an activity that Musorgsky warmly encouraged (copies are extant of two of Kutuzov's historical plays, *Hashish* and *Vasily Shuisky*, with the composer's detailed advice in delicate calligraphy in the margins). Kutuzov was eager to train himself in dramatic technique, with its devices of suspense and the well-timed resolution. But he intuitively placed the playwright outside the action, containing and managing its effects. In his poetic *Songs and Dances of Death* he framed the scenarios in the same way, opening and closing each episode with a poet's commentary on events, along the lines of a Greek chorus. Like the later Symbolists, Kutuzov saw death as a mystery, a passage, a seduction into another world, and the poet as midwife to the event. Musorgsky was no stranger to this idea; the final act of *Khovanshchina* is just such a passage. But the Old Believers had deep religious faith and thus had somewhere to go. Musorgsky wished to communicate the fact that the threatened mortals in *Songs and Dances* have only terror.

Terror of such incandescent quality must preserve the present tense. There can be no survivors left to frame the story, to comment on it or to round out the scene. Just as the songs in *The Nursery* must be performed as a child's ongoing experience (not as *recollections* of experience, which is the more common structure of an art song), so these *Songs and Dances* had to be, in a cruel way, largely dances. Only activity that is alive and moving at the moment of singing is vulnerable enough to die; the cutting off of real activity is everywhere more terrifying than the interruption of a merely recollected act. Since music is tremendously good at the present tense – one could even say that this is all music does – Musorgsky set out in his songs to restore all the terror that the poet-playwright had smoothed away.

The composer did not alter very much in Kutuzov's texts as he put them to music, but what he did change was chilling. He sheared off the outer frame of the poems and moved verbs into the present tense. Little was left of the "lyrical reminiscence," which was too sentimental and mediated for what Musorgsky had in mind. In each song there is a point, usually a chord, where Death unambiguously triumphs over life. Although some delaying tactics are tried (the mother in "Lullaby" holds Death a bit at bay with her desperate pleas, and several times at the end of "Trepak" the snowstorm, a sign of life, breaks into the freezing peasant's benumbed consciousness), the final outcome is never in doubt. To transmit all the terror of Death's victory, the composer had to insure that the touch of death ended the song *and the singer*. No one could be left alive to sum up the situation. Anything less would be simply a song *about* death – like songs *about* childhood or sung *to* children. (Tchaikovsky's sixteen "Children's Songs," Op. 54 [1883], are in this conventional vein.) As always, Musorgsky insisted on getting at experience from the inside. The hero of the *Songs and Dances* cycle, "She," would not spare the narrator. Such song-writing is Musorgsky's aural equivalent to Vereshchagin's uncanny canvases showing death as all-encompassing process. It took the drama out of the lyric poet's comforting hands.

By the mid-1870s, Musorgsky was well practiced in these musical discussions of loss and death. Art and life inspired one another – but where expertise was gained in art, coping became increasingly difficult in life. Events in the composer's daily round become less well documented. He had switched from well-heeled hosts and professional musician friends to more irregular, and less "writerly," comrades; one begins to feel, in the accounts left by his old friends (letter-and-memoir-writers all), a rising sense of anxiety and patronizing concern. Others grew up; Musorgsky was still a truant from school. Ilya Repin, who at this time was still devoted to Stasov, left the grimmest portrait. In the summer of 1875, Repin was waiting for Stasov in Paris. When Stasov finally appeared his mood was buoyant, but, Repin writes in his memoirs:

> one thought gnawed at his heart: he could not stop thinking of Musorgsky! "Oh, what is happening to our poor Musoryanin?!" More than once, Vladimir Vasilievich [Stasov] had to go to the rescue of his genius friend, who, in his absence, sank to the very bottom . . . Oh, how many times, upon his return from abroad, would Vladimir Vasilievich, after great difficulty, finally find him in some basement establishment, nearly in rags . . . Vladimir Vasilievich would continually bombard all his close friends with letters, asking for news about Musorgsky, about the mysterious stranger he had now become, for nobody knew where Musorgsky had hidden himself. (MR, 73)

"Hidden himself": Repin's naive sentence prompts us to consider the trajectory of Musorgsky's homes. For over half his life, Modest had been the favorite son, nurtured at the center of an extended family of well-to-do rural nobility. As a cadet and a young officer in St. Petersburg, his mother's solicitous services and devotion were always present. From 1864 to 1865 he lived in the "commune," and from 1865 to 1868 with his brother and sister-in-law. But at that point when most adults fix themselves into families, he began to be ever more peripheral. Even Filaret appears to have lost hope and lost track. "After 1868," he wrote, and rather coldly, in response to Stasov's summons for a memoir, "I am unable to provide exact information on where and how Modest lived" (MR, 27). Wealthier friends (the Shilovskys, then the Opochinins) offered refuge for a while, but after the *Boris* period passed, this option appears to have been less and less available to him. Beginning in 1875, sketches and photographs of Musorgsky, who had always been so fastidiously dressed and groomed, show him looking for the first time unkempt in a way that could not be entirely disguised for the camera.

Musorgsky could not afford decent lodgings on his salary alone. However, his housemates did not last. Sharing rooms with Rimsky-Korsakov in 1871–72 was for one season only, a short-term arrangement fully in the order of things; Rimsky's marriage to Nadezhda Purgold had long been expected in their circle. But the loss of Golenishchev-Kutuzov in 1875 was a shock that Musorgsky took very hard. At one level, the younger man moved out to get married: what could be more natural? But there are hints of more desperate and dependent moments.

For one thing, the separation took a long time. The two men had become extremely close (exactly along what lines we cannot know, although the creative bond was intense and reciprocal). Count Kutuzov, who was well off, could leave for one of his rural properties at will – and often did. Musorgsky had nowhere else to go. Dobrovensky suggests in his biography that Kutuzov's mother must have looked askance at this intimacy and pressured her son to relocate; in fact, the Countess did call her son frequently to their country residences, and he could set up at one of several addresses in the capital as well.[12] One can sympathize with the poet; Musorgsky must not have been easy company. When Kutuzov returned to the city during the spring and summer of 1875, he did not always summon Musorgsky to join him. Once or twice, the composer was too proud to ask.

During this year, letters between mutual friends of both men hint at ghastly humiliating episodes, which Musorgsky's own correspondence masks over. Liudmila Shestakova, for example, writes Nikolsky in June 1875: "Poor Musorgsky: they are driving him from his apartment; things are bad . . ."[13] Musorgsky himself, writing to Stasov in Paris over a month later, is painstakingly casual in explaining his new residence: "How I – your *modest* Musoryanin – am getting along you can see by the address written above on this bit of paper: a simple matter – Arseny took the apartment key with him, and I, because of this, am boarding at the expense of Naumov, my very kind friend" (L, 301).

Naumov's niece, however, left another account of how Musorgsky ended up at his final lodging.

> Musorgsky, hopelessly in arrears in his rent, came home to find his suitcase and things piled beside the outer door, which was locked. With this suitcase and empty pockets, he wandered for a long time at night through the St. Petersburg streets, finally sitting down to rest on one of the stone lions decorating some important building on the Neva Embankment. Here, meditating despondently on his situation, an idea suddenly occurred to him: "What am I thinking of? Why, on the other side is my dear friend Naumov! To him!" In the middle of the night, the Naumov door was opened for the homeless M[odest] P[etrovich].[14]

There is much in the niece's account that sounds apocryphal – for example, the detail about "sitting down on the stone lion," so clearly reminiscent of the destitute hero of Pushkin's famous St. Petersburg poem from the 1830s, "The Bronze Horseman." But without question Musorgsky's condition was unstable, both financially and psychologically. Later that August, he patched together a face-saving story for Kutuzov, writing to him in the country and pleading loss of a house key to explain the present arrangement with Naumov ("for, as you know, I am afraid to stay *alone*" [L, 303]). When it became clear, however, after several months of uncertainty, that the Count planned to marry a seventeen-year-old girl and thus move out permanently, Musorgsky's immediate response was desperate.

"So much disgust and dissipation, such huge hopes and desires (terrible to utter!) – but you, my dear, allowed yourself to behave badly," he wrote to Kutuzov at the beginning of December 1875 (L, 320). "What has happened to you?" At the end of that month, in a letter marked "At night, 'without sun'" (the composer was partial to letter-writing in the deep of night, which might explain the tone), Musorgsky wrote:

> In this silence, in the peace that comes to all minds, all consciences and all desires – I, who adore you, I alone threaten you. My threat has no anger in it. It is quiet, like sleep without nightmares. I stand before you neither as a goblin nor a ghost . . . You have chosen your path, go! You disdained everything: the empty hint, the jesting sorrowfulness of friendship, my confidence in you and in your thoughts – and in *your creations*; you disdained a cry from the heart – so, disdain it! It is not for me to judge. (L, 322)

As a postscript to this letter, Musorgsky quoted back to the poet the opening words of the poet's own poem, the first in that beautiful, bleak cycle *Without Sun* which they had co-created in 1874: "'A cramped room, quiet, familiar . . .'" He then added: "do not curse me, my friend." The poem, "Within Four Walls," reads in full: "A cramped room, quiet, familiar; dense and unanswering shadow, deep thoughts, a mournful song. But there is sacred hope in my beating heart, time flies quickly, minute by minute, my motionless gaze fixed on distant happiness; so many doubts, so much endurance; there it is, my night, my lonely night."

Five days later, Musorgsky turned to Stasov. Stasov's support in these matters – in all matters – was all too ready and absolute whenever the composer broke down. "The thing is, my dear, a young lad has gone astray," Musorgsky wrote jauntily to his mentor (L, 322–23).

> And he who has strayed is none other than M. Arseny Golenishchev-Kutuzov-Count – and this is the way it is: he has decided to get married! And this is no joke, he says it's the *real thing*. So yet another "goes home to the village on furlough," never to return. God! . . . I

scolded Arseny and was extremely rude to the aforementioned
Arseny. He asked me to visit his fiancée (whom I don't know) – but
I'm *not going*; I would have to lie. I don't want him to do what he's
doing – and I won't go, that's all. He says he fell in love with her – all
the same, I *won't go*. I mustn't. Such things make me want to work
more than ever. And I'm left alone – so, I'll be alone. You have to die
alone anyway, not everyone can cross over with me . . . But it's a pity
about Arseny . . .

That this petulance and passion is evidence of a broken heart, there
can be no doubt. That we again see in Musorgsky the character traits of
those literary prototypes to which he was so often drawn can hardly be
disputed: the heaviness and helplessness of an Oblomov, the wariness
of a Podkolyosin, Gogol's confirmed bachelor in *Marriage*. But the
tragedy, it would seem, was as much a spatial and family one as it was
specifically sexual. Musorgsky had so few places left to look for a home.

By April, the composer had made up with the new young Countess
Golenishcheva-Kutuzova. As a gesture of apology and reconciliation,
he dedicated to her on her birthday the "Dance of the Persian Slaves"
from *Khovanshchina*. But from then on, it appears, he never doubted
that he would "cross over" alone.

In the summer of 1873, that aspect of Viktor Hartmann's dying
most bitter for Musorgsky to recall was his own behavior at the time of
his friend's heart trouble, several months before the end.[15] The two
men were walking together down a St. Petersburg street. As
Musorgsky recorded the event in a letter to Stasov, suddenly, "dear
Vityushka leaned against a wall and turned pale. Knowing our brethren from my own experience, I asked him (*calmly*): 'What's happened?' – 'I can't breathe,' answered Vityushka . . . I (*still calmly*) told
Vityushka: 'Rest a bit, my dear friend, and then we'll go on.' That was
all that was said, about something that has hidden forever beneath the
earth a person who was dear to us. What a fool man is, in general!"
Later in the letter Musorgsky expands on his folly, and on the fraudu-
lence of reconciliation. "The wise comfort us fools in these cases,"
Musorgsky wrote, adding bitterly:

"He" [they say] no longer exists, but all the things he had time to accomplish do exist and will continue to exist, and are there many people who have such a happy lot – not to be forgotten? Again, that beef cutlet (with horseradish to make us cry) made out of human self-love! To hell with your wisdom! If "he" has not lived in vain, but *created*, what a scoundrel one would have to be to reconcile oneself with the delightful "consolation" that now "*he has ceased to create.*" There is not and should not be any peace here, there is not and should not be any consolation – that would be flaccid of us. If nature is only playing the coquette with a human being . . . [then I will treat her like one,] then I will trust her as little as possible and keep a sharp watch over her . . . But there's the fool again, what's the point of anger, when it's impotent.

For all the magnificent skills Musorgsky had acquired, his contest with death had ended in a draw.

6   Beyond tragedy: the final years

Musorgsky's final half-decade, 1876–81, is poor in documents. What testimony we have suggests a life of increasing material deprivation, self-delusion, self-confidence, and an astonishing resilience. All four factors are manifest in a now-famous episode related by Vasily Bertenson, a medical student in St. Petersburg, whose elder brother Lev attended Musorgsky on his deathbed.

In March 1880, the younger Bertenson was in charge of organizing a benefit concert for his fellow students-in-training. "Modest Petrovich was an outstanding accompanist," Bertenson recalled.

> Although poor as Job himself, when it came to charity concerts he would accept no money for his work . . . Even though I had boldly announced to all participants that Musorgsky was going to be our accompanist . . . at that moment I was unwillingly deceiving them. The fact was that the author of *Boris Godunov* . . . was rumored to be drinking hard; therefore, asking him three weeks in advance to participate in a concert meant that there was no way of knowing if, on the designated day, one could rely on him . . .
>
> As a special attraction, I was fortunate enough to obtain, in addition to artists from the Russian opera, the splendid tenor Ravelli, from the Italian opera . . . The day before the concert [5 April 1880], Ravelli told me he wanted to meet his accompanist, and for this purpose he asked Musorgsky to come to his house the following day, as early as possible, for a rehearsal. The day before, I had received Musorgsky's agreement to participate; happy at having found him

sober, I went to him again to fulfill Ravelli's request. To my horror
I found Musorgsky hopelessly in his cups. Babbling on, for some
reason in French, he assured me that there was no need to go see the
Italian, that he would manage, etc.

None of my pleadings had any effect on him: with a drunkard's
stubbornness he kept repeating: "Non, monsieur, non: maintenant
c'est impossible. Ce soir je serai exacte [sic]." Musorgsky was then
living in a small unkempt room. There was a bottle of vodka on a dirty
table and some scraps of miserable food. When I took my leave, he
stood up with great difficulty, but nevertheless saw me to the door.
Making a low bow, perhaps not totally worthy of Louis XIV but utterly
amazing for a person so completely "tight," he added, "Donc, à ce soir!"

So I went back to my tenor and told him that I had not found
Musorgsky at home. After much persuasion I managed to convince
him not to pull out of the concert . . . assuring him that the
accompanist was a marvelous, extremely capable one . . . Then I
immediately dispatched a friend to fetch Musorgsky and keep watch
over him. Promptly at seven o'clock, Musorgsky was in Kononov
Hall, where the concert was to take place. Unfortunately, in the green
room Musorgsky continually helped himself to various drinks,
which were right at hand, and got more and more intoxicated.
Suddenly, my tenor, trying a roulade, discovered that his voice had
lowered, and therefore decided to sing all his repertoire half a tone
or, if necessary, a whole tone lower.

That was the last straw! I rushed to Musorgsky and asked him if
he could perform this service for Ravelli. Rising up with a certain
gallantry, Musorgsky reassured me with: "Of course, why not?" also
in French (apparently Musorgsky spoke only French with cultured
people as soon as he was even a little bit tipsy). To reassure the tenor,
he suggested that he sing through his entire repertoire in *mezza voce*.
Musorgsky, who was undoubtedly hearing the Italian songs sung by
Ravelli for the first time, so charmed the Italian with his talented
rendition and his ability to play in any key, that the latter started to
hug him, saying, "*Che artista!*"

Both Ravelli and Musorgsky enjoyed an immense success . . .[1]

To put this horrific episode in context, three basic questions must
be asked of the final years. Where did Musorgsky live? What did he live

on? What was he working on – and was anyone sympathetic to this work? After *Boris Godunov*, Musorgsky ceased to be a public personality in any important way; once again, his friends became his major court of judgment, and private correspondence again becomes the biographer's primary mode of access to his life. Yet even on this "unofficial" terrain, the composer's letters do not correlate with memoir accounts. The more disappointing and depleted the reality, the more hopeful and effusive are Musorgsky's accounts of his activity and future plans. It appears that his new friends (with the exception of the loyal Golenishchev-Kutuzov) were not much given to writing letters. Rimsky-Korsakov and other longstanding musical friends who stayed in contact out of love or duty dismissed Musorgsky among themselves as "almost lost," "hopeless," "writing nothing but rubbish." Meanwhile, lofty-sounding letters from "Musinka" could not be squared with actual unnerving encounters. "I urged him to come to our *dacha* for the summer," Rimsky-Korsakov wrote in May 1880 to Stasov in Rome (L, 403–04). "At first he was evasive . . . I went to him in the morning, it was about noon, he was still in bed and was vomiting nearly every moment; but he seems little disturbed by this, as if it were the most ordinary thing. He says that this is very good."

Was Musorgsky in deep denial? Or so chemically addicted that he no longer shared the same world with Rimsky-Korsakov, conservatory professor, or Vladimir Stasov, Imperial librarian on a research tour through Europe? Perhaps such behavior was an extension of his aristocratic code, which mandated that one not complain and try not to notice those traits in oneself that could not be respected – or changed. Or perhaps it was all much simpler, an act of reconciliation. We must begin with the material facts of his life, if we are to untangle the confusing currents of pity, shock, and recrimination that followed Musorgsky's death on 16 March 1881, his forty-second birthday.

First, his lodgings. After Kutuzov's marriage in the spring of 1876, Musorgsky sought refuge with Pavel Naumov, a retired naval officer, theatre-lover, and indefatigable *bon vivant*. The arrangement, more

22 Musorgsky with Pavel Naumov, 1880, in whose household the composer lived
intermittently from 1875 to 1879

like an open invitation, continued on and off for four years, and it was
not bad: Musorgsky had companionship, a room, access to a piano. In
several letters, the composer tried to interest Stasov and Liudmila
Shestakova in his new friend, but to no avail. For one thing, there were
irregularities: Naumov, who had a young son, had squandered several
inheritances and now, estranged from his wife, was living openly with
his sister-in-law (Musorgsky dedicated a song to her, "The Misunderstood One," in December 1875). Then there was the assumption, not
unfounded, that Musorgsky found Naumov's drinking habits all too
congenial. In August 1878, after a summer of almost total silence,

Musorgsky turned up at Shestakova's "looking dreadful and staying quite a long time," as the frightened elderly woman wrote to Stasov (L, 371). "In order to save him and to protect myself," she continued, "I wrote him a letter asking him not to call on me when suffering from his 'nervous irritation' (as he calls it) . . . and yesterday evening, my dear Musinka appeared in *complete* order, and gave me his word never to distress me again . . . If only there were some way to pull him away from Naumov, I think he might be rescued definitively." Musorgsky moved out of the Naumovs' in 1879 (the wife, it appears, had returned); from then on he had several addresses, none with a piano. Among the worst was the room Vasily Bertenson saw in March 1880, seeking out his accompanist for the charity concert.

What was Musorgsky living on? His possible sources of income were the following: the revenues due him from his Karevo property; royalties for music published or performed; fees for accompanying at musical events; and the pittance of a salary he received as a clerk. As regards the first, there is only one extant letter, dated November 1876, from Musorgsky to his steward-tenant at Karevo, Alexander Morozov. In it Musorgsky pleads courteously with Morozov and his wife "not to forget about me and send me as much money as possible by December . . . and along with this, tell me how the farming arrangement goes, and why you are concerned about the land sales" (L, 350). The tone of the letter is hardly that of a landlord with any power to enforce his property rights, and there is no evidence that the Morozovs sent anything at all.

There was a trickle of income from the music. After the 1874 premiere, there were twenty-two more performances given of *Boris Godunov* through October 1882, often to full or nearly-full houses. (For the 1876 revival, large cuts were made in the opera, including the entire final Kromy scene. Although Musorgsky apparently approved of the omissions and – here as during the premiere – was grateful for a conscientious production, Stasov was outraged and wrote an angry public letter.[2]) The composer received a small fraction of these box-office receipts. There had also been the sale of *The Nursery* to Bessel.

In the summer of 1877, Musorgsky negotiated through Dmitry Stasov, a lawyer, with Jurgenson Publishers over rights to *Songs and Dances of Death* and to settings of several poems by Alexei K. Tolstoy. The deal fell through.

Many years after Musorgsky's death, in 1909, the music critic Mikhail Ivanov (who wrote one of the first obituaries in March 1881) summed up this sad state of affairs, which he felt had been misrepresented by Rimsky-Korsakov in his memoirs. "Musorgsky, incidentally, was not, even in his last years, a true 'professional composer,'" Ivanov wrote. "He was only a 'professional accompanist.' Accompanists can now receive good money for their work . . . but that was not the case earlier, when the accompanist could not bring in a penny. Everyone appeared on the stage 'as an honor.' Musorgsky was no exception."[3] During the 1870s, Musorgsky himself had hoped otherwise. With his customary optimism, he wrote to Stasov in June 1876: "So far, fate has preserved me. From the present *overall* state of affairs, however, one can hardly expect anything. Recently I've been working a lot at the piano, and I've come to the conclusion that if I'm destined to earn my daily bread by clattering, I'll manage" (L, 338). This did not come to pass, not the least because Musorgsky, as we have seen, found it extremely difficult to demand money from others. He had never entered into the mercantile spirit of his time. In the terms of Goncharov's novel that so impressed him as a young man, he was an Oblomov in the age of Stolz.

Now to Musorgsky's final source of income: his senior clerking job at the Forestry Department. His starting salary in that post, back in 1869, had been 450 rubles annually, about $350. Although Musorgsky had no bureaucratic ambition, still, by trudging through the ranks, he was promoted to "collegiate counsellor" in May 1878; his annual salary was up to 1,200 rubles, or almost a thousand dollars. By that time, however, increasingly frequent absences for "illness" put this job in jeopardy. In March 1878, Musorgsky was devastated by the death of his intimate friend, the great bass Osip Petrov (who, at age sixty-seven, had created the role of the drunken friar Varlaam in the

Boris premiere four years earlier); this fresh loss triggered a drinking bout that lasted well into the summer. Musorgsky's old circle of musical colleagues now began to mobilize on his behalf. Balakirev had a friend in the Department of Government Control, Terty Filippov, an expert on folk songs and an enthusiast of the new Russian music. At some professional risk, Filippov managed to get Musorgsky transferred to his department, into an absolute sinecure which, although temporary and poorly paid, required him to do no work at all ("I am the servant of artists," Filippov admitted). The chief of the Forestry division – that same chief to whom Musorgsky had professed such loyalty in the summer of 1873 that he would not take off and visit Liszt – scribbled in the margins of the transfer notice: "Very glad!"

When this temporary and fictitious employment came to an end in December 1879, Stasov wrote Balakirev an urgent note three days into the new year: "Without fail I want to do something for Musorgsky. He is sinking. Since January 1, he has been left without a post and without means of any sort. Little wonder if he should begin to drink even more" (L, 401). Balakirev suggested a benefit concert. Filippov and the others came up with what seemed like a more reliable long-term solution: to pool their funds and guarantee Musorgsky a composing "pension" of 100 rubles a month, on condition that he finish *Khovanshchina*. Other donors came up with an additional 80 rubles per month for *Sorochintsy Fair*. By this time Musorgsky was no longer in a position to refuse "alarming his friends," as he had been able to do in the summer of 1867 when he declined a similar offer of help. But his gallantry remained. "Cordial thanks for your good news," he wrote Stasov on 16 January 1880 (L, 401–02). "In spite of small misfortunes, I have not and will not give way to faintheartedness. You know my motto: 'Be bold and dare! Forward! To new shores!' – and it has remained unchanged."

The morality of these last-minute subsidies to the "sinking" composer has long been a matter of dispute. Why did his well-heeled friends not come to his aid earlier? Could they have done so – and in what form, given that Musorgsky was, after all, an adult and a man with some pride? Had he not, in a sense, "chosen" a bohemian way of life, not uncommon among artists? In any event, this was not an era that offered welfare or drug counseling; problems such as poverty or alcoholism were concealed within the home, and Musorgsky had no home. Could the pressure and shame of those subsidies even have increased the disorderliness of his life?

Such matters are difficult to evaluate. But the composer's final years became part of the mythology surrounding the Russian mystique of strong drink – and on that topic, some speculations have emerged of more recent vintage. In 1968, Venedikt Erofeev (who would also die of alcoholism) produced an underground bestseller, *Moskva-Petushki*, that promoted drunkenness as Russia's lifesaving national virtue. Cast in the style of one long monologue in *delirium tremens*, it includes this psychologically astute passage (conflating the roles of Stasov and Rimsky):

> And old Modest Musorgsky. My good God, do you know how he wrote his immortal opera *Khovanshchina*? It's laughter and grief. Modest Musorgsky lies dead drunk in a ditch, and Nikolai Rimsky-Korsakov comes by dressed in a smoking jacket and carrying a bamboo walking-stick. Nikolai Rimsky-Korsakov stops, tickles Modest with his walking-stick and says: "Get up! Go wash yourself and sit down and finish writing your divine opera *Khovanshchina*!" And so they sit there, Nikolai Rimsky-Korsakov in an armchair, crossing one leg over the other and with his top-hat in his outstretched hand. While opposite him sits Modest Musorgsky, all limp, unshaven, hunched over a bench, sweating, writing down notes. Modest at the bench desperately wants to tie one on – who cares about notes! But Nikolai Rimsky-Korsakov, with his top-hat in his outstretched hand, won't let him ... But as soon as the door closes behind Rimsky-Korsakov, Modest throws down his immortal opera *Khovanshchina* and it's thump – back into the ditch. And later he gets up and ties one on, and again – thump ...[4]

Reading this passage in Erofeev's hallucinatory novel, one recalls what Musorgsky wrote to Stasov in June 1872, in his first flush of excitement over *Khovanshchina*: "Public benefactors will seek to glorify themselves . . . but the people groan, and to stifle their groans they drink like the devil, and groan worse than ever: *haven't moved!*"

Against this material and psychological background, in lodgings that lacked a piano and in increasing isolation, Musorgsky continued to work during these final five years. What was the direction of his musical development? Some clues have been lost. The composer spent the summer of 1880, for example, with a relative of Golenishchev-Kutuzov's in the country, and the housekeeper later tossed onto a bonfire the heap of papers and music manuscripts she found in Musorgsky's rooms. We know that he made progress on his two operas "under commission," and that he composed several incidental songs. However slender this corpus, Golenishchev-Kutuzov, in his memoirs, sees Musorgsky's final years not as a decline but as a liberation and rebirth. The song cycles of the mid-1870s, the lyricism in *Khovanshchina* (its twenty embedded songs, around which the entire opera is structured), and the "clear, simple, gentle poetry" being composed for *Sorochintsy Fair* were all an indication, in Kutuzov's view, that Musorgsky was finally breaking away from the "delusions" encouraged in him by his *kuchkist* confrères. Free of those hectoring mentors, Musorgsky the improviser was always lyrical, Kutuzov insisted; his nature "constantly drew him toward a pure, ideal poetry and beauty, toward a spiritual, perfect world."[5]

Other evidence, however, attests to a continuity between Musorgsky's last years and the radicalism of his youth. Stasov continued doggedly to stand guard at the portal of Musorgsky's talent. And the composer continued to turn to him gratefully, even if he was not always disposed to accept the advice he received. "Our *Khovanshchina* is finished, except for a little piece in the final scene of the self-immolation," he wrote to Stasov in August 1880 (L, 405). "But tell me, what should I do with my devils in *Sorochintsy* – what clothes should I dress them in? . . . What would a drunken Ukrainian village lad see in his dream? . . . I beg your good help. The scene of the Black God is turning out well, but . . . a senseless setting is an abomination for me, and a senseless portrayal of a human dream fantasy all the more so, and furthermore a drunken fantasy – help me."

There is also some indication that Stasov's shrill, pontificating style continued to surface in the mature Musorgsky, at least in certain states. The composer Mikhail Ippolitov-Ivanov (1859–1935), a student of Rimsky-Korsakov, professor at the Moscow Conservatory and the one who, in 1931, completed the musical setting of Musorgsky's abandoned *Marriage*, was nineteen years old when he first met Modest Petrovich in 1879. "He would usually talk about himself and would attack us, the younger generation," Ippolitov-Ivanov recalled fifty years later, one year before his own death.

> "You young people," he said to me during a walk, "sitting in your conservatory, don't want to know anything beyond your *cantus firmus*; do you think that the Zaremba formula 'the minor key is our original sin but the major key is our redemption,' or that 'rest, movement, and rest again,' exhausts everything? No, my dears, in my opinion if you want to sin, then go ahead and sin; if there is movement, then there is no return to rest; one must go forward, destroying everything." While saying this he proudly tossed his head. (MR, 135)

Most likely, all these accounts are accurate. During his final years, Musorgsky had not the luxury of working out a consistent musical philosophy – and indeed, so few people took him seriously, he can hardly be held responsible for one.

In January 1879, Rimsky-Korsakov conducted the premiere performance of the scene in Pimen's cell from *Boris Godunov*, which had been omitted from all performances of the opera. Thus Musorgsky reappeared briefly as a public personality, open to the judgment of the musical press. Reviews were poor. One unsigned essay called it a scene "without great merit, and its length is tiring . . . In the theatre it might prove interesting, but in Kononov Hall, Mr. Musorgsky's excerpt passed without leaving a trace."[6] Then there was the conservative critic Nikolai Soloviev. "What delightful poetry and what drab music!" Soloviev remarked, appreciating the fact that Pushkin's verses had been set almost without change.

> Just think, Mr. Musorgsky could not come up with anything more witty for this scene than to give the orchestra a figure from ordinary five-finger piano exercises. Knowing Mr. Musorgsky's realistic inclination, one might think that he wanted to present Pimen practicing the piano rather than writing his chronicle . . . To what delicacy might this scene of Mr. Musorgsky's be compared? I compare it outright to an emaciated and partially rotten oyster on which a few drops of lemon juice have been sprinkled, in the form of a tam-tam and a church chorus, to make it more pleasant to swallow.[7]

The composer – himself no stranger to culinary metaphors – left no record of his reaction to this extravagant insult.

The two ongoing opera projects moved forward in uneasy tandem. Musorgsky had begun *Sorochintsy Fair* in 1874, as comic relief from the historical gravity of *Khovanshchina* ("two heavyweights in succession might be crushing," as he wrote in July to one supportive lady friend [L, 278]). But the projects seemed to obstruct rather than complement one another. In 1876, work on the Ukrainian opera picked up – largely due to the advice and encouragement of the magnificent bass Osip Petrov, for whom the lead role was intended. Musorgsky participated actively in Petrov's fifty-year jubilee, observed that year, which became a celebration of Russian music from Glinka to the present. When Petrov died in 1878, eyewitnesses at the funeral remarked how Musorgsky sobbed convulsively over the coffin: "I've lost everything, I've lost the sole support of my bitter life."[8] The comic opera was temporarily shelved. When the "subsidies" began in 1880, only *Khovanshchina* was anywhere near completion.

The major interruption in Musorgsky's composing during 1879 was his concert tour. The idea for this joint venture belonged to Darya Leonova, a fifty-year-old contralto who in 1873 had sung the role of the Hostess at the Inn in the three concert scenes from *Boris*. Kindly, a bit naive, with genuine talent but also with a fading diva's inflated sense of her audience, Leonova hoped that a visit to the Russian provinces with a repertory of opera excerpts, romances, and solo piano pieces would crown her own career and inspire (or at least stimulate) Musorgsky, whom she deeply respected. The planned tour, scheduled from July through October, was to cover twelve cities in southern Russia and the Crimea, important provincial centers such as Poltava, Odessa, Sevastopol, Yalta, and Tver. Musorgsky calculated that it would clear at least a thousand rubles profit. He was to function both as accompanist and as soloist, in a program that was largely Russian vocal music but with his own works – often in piano reduction or keyboard improvisation – very well represented. Musorgsky, who before this time had never traveled beyond St. Petersburg, Moscow, and his native Pskov province, was as delighted as a child.

The news did not please his musical friends. "What's happening to Modest is terrible," Balakirev wrote Liudmila Shestakova in mid-June 1879. "If you could only disrupt this tour with Leonova, you would be doing a good deed. On the one hand, you would release him from the shameful role he wishes to assume; and besides, Modest and Leonova are running a big risk. What if his blood should start flowing from someplace, as once happened at your home? . . . And his ruin is likely, because Leonova, naturally, will not fail to exploit him – it's cheaper for her this way! – but for him, it's simply shameful" (L, 376). The southern tour was not "disrupted," and on 21 July, Leonova and her pianist set out for the first city on their circuit, Poltava.

The overall success of this ambitious four-month tour is difficult to judge. Without question there were several local triumphs. The provincial nobility was unexpectedly eager and musically literate, and the two "artists of the Imperial Theatres" – as Leonova and Musorgsky had a right to call themselves on the promotion posters – were frequently invited into private homes for additional music-making and lavish receptions. Musorgsky sent long letters back to St. Petersburg, many to the Naumovs but some to Stasov and Shestakova as well, ecstatic about the scenery, the sunsets, the weather, Leonova's singing, and characteristically making light of the occasional poor turnout. ("The receipts are good, although less than we expected," he wrote to the Naumovs at the end of July, regarding the second concert in Poltava; "still, the artistic triumph was *absolute*" [L, 378].)

There were some low moments as well. In Yalta at the beginning of September, the traveling pair was caught without accommodations or advance publicity at the height of the tourist season. Billeted in a bug-infested shack, they suffered a miserable first concert. At the time, Stasov's (illegitimate) daughter, Sophia Fortunato, was managing the best hotel in Yalta, the Grand Hôtel de Russie; when she discovered by chance who was in town, she rushed to the concert site and was distressed to see almost no audience. "During the first intermission I ran to the green room," she recalled in her memoirs forty years later. "M. P. was sitting in an armchair, his arms hanging at his sides, looking like a wounded bird. The absence of any real audience had obviously depressed him very much" (MR, 41). Madame Fortunato, a devoted admirer of Musorgsky, immediately arranged to have the two artists moved into a luxury suite of the Grand Hôtel, which had a magnificent reception hall and grand piano. She advertised their presence among her patrons, and the second concert was a great success. Musorgsky spent a week in Yalta under these blissful conditions. From his suite he wrote lengthy, purring letters back home, such as this one in mid-September to Nadezhda Stasova, Madame Fortunato's aunt: "And I, like cheese melting in butter, am luxuriating in Yalta under the patronage of the enchantress Sofia Vladimirovna . . . What air! what surroundings! what sea!" (L, 395). To Stasov, who held the usual big-city prejudices about the low cultural level of Russia's outlying regions, Musorgsky made a bold statement: "To you, my dear, I will say one thing: that Peter[sburg] is not such a splendid connoisseur of the Russian provinces" (L, 392).

In her memoirs written ten years after Musorgsky's death, Darya Leonova captures the childlike vulnerability of her co-artist during these years. "He was not an ordinary man," she wrote. "He never acknowledged intrigues; he could not believe that an educated, intelligent person would wish to harm or do a despicable thing to another person" (MR, 125). But for all the personal compatibility between singer and pianist and the rich impressions received, the southern tour was not a financial success. Upon their return to St. Petersburg, Leonova invited Musorgsky – now fully retired from government service – to work as accompanist in her makeshift school for singing. "He had great hopes for this enterprise," she noted in her memoirs, "as it would allow him to earn a living; his means were very, very limited." The matronly Leonova (who became the final "Agafya Matveyevna" figure in Musorgsky's life) possessed the sort of provisioning instincts toward which the composer had always gravitated so effortlessly.

Rimsky-Korsakov had harsh words for this joint project as well. "Leonova was very fond of talking of herself, her merits and her preeminence," Rimsky wrote in his memoirs.

> She was a talented artiste who had once had a fine contralto voice; but in reality she had never had any training and was therefore scarcely capable of teaching the technique of singing. Musorgsky's association with her was an advertisement for Leonova to a certain degree ... He gave rather much of his time to instruction in these classes, teaching even elementary theory and composing some trios and quartets, with horrible part-writing, as exercises for Leonova's pupils. His function in her classes was, of course, not to be envied; still, he either didn't notice this or tried not to.[9]

During the summer of 1880, Musorgsky turned down invitations from his sterner musical friends in favor of spending those months with Leonova and her amiable husband at their cottage in Oranienbaum outside of St. Petersburg. According to fellow summer residents, much feasting, drinking, and piano-playing went on at the Leonova *dacha*. There was some work as well: the last manuscripts of *Khovanshchina* are dated August 1880, by which time the opera was complete in piano-vocal score except for the end of Act 2 and the Old Believers' chorus at the final curtain. Autumn of that year yielded little, but there was one bright and curious moment.

In late November, excerpts from *Khovanshchina* were performed at a Free Music School concert conducted by Rimsky-Korsakov. The gorgeous "Dance of the Persian Slave Girls" from Act 4 was included on the program, but as the concert date approached, there was still no full score – and Musorgsky could not be found. Rimsky-Korsakov sat down and orchestrated the Dance on the spot. The piece was a tremendous success with the public; Musorgsky, exuberant, was called out several times. As Rimsky's wife Nadezhda later recalled, Musorgsky afterwards repeated over and over, "with absolutely childlike naiveté," how glad he was that it had turned out this way, "that he would have orchestrated the piece himself exactly as Korsakov had done," and that he was "absolutely astonished" how Rimsky had divined his intentions, even though a large number of changes had been made in the harmony.[10] Granted, Rimsky's wife, in the 1890s when these recollections were made, had some stake in remembering the event this way after her husband had put in such thankless labor over their deceased friend's manuscripts. Still, the scene does not ring wholly false. Musorgsky, for all his stubbornness, was always enormously grateful for any public act of inclusion and recognition.

In the winter and spring of 1881, the Grim Reaper moved over Russia with special visibility. Dostoevsky died at the end of January. Tsar Alexander II was assassinated by a terrorist's bomb in early March. In between those two very public deaths came the beginning of the end for Musorgsky as well. On 11 February, he turned up at Darya Leonova's in a terrible state. As she later described it, "he told me that he had no place to go, that nothing remained for him but to go live in the streets, that he had no further resources and there was no other way out of his situation. What could I do? I tried to calm him down, saying that although I did not have much, everything I had I would share with him" (MR, 125). That evening, after accompanying a singing pupil of theirs at a musical gathering, Musorgsky had what appears to have been a stroke. He recovered, spent the night at Leonova's, but the following morning had another seizure and lost consciousness. Thoroughly frightened, Leonova contacted Stasov and Filippov. The search began for a hospital that could take the sick man in.

In 1922, Lev Bertenson (1850–1929), a surgeon and amateur musician, recalled those distant and frantic days (MR, 131–32). Cui, Stasov, Rimsky-Korsakov, and Borodin had turned to him immediately as a "friend of music" who could find Musorgsky – who was still unconscious – a decent place, despite his destitution and low civil rank. At the time, Bertenson was only a junior staff physician, working at two hospitals, with no administrative influence. When he inquired at the Nikolaev Military Hospital, the most likely option of the two, the head physician reprimanded him for asking the impossible. Then, softening in the face of his young colleague's despair, the head doctor agreed to accept the sick man into the hospital as the "civilian orderly of the intern Bertenson" – if, he added gently, the composer's high-ranking friends were willing to accept such a "lofty rank." The sick man was promptly placed in a spacious private room, with excellent care and an officer's rations. Friends began to arrive that very day, and from then on Musorgsky was almost never alone. He frequently told his visitors that he felt as if he were in his own home, surrounded by his family. After several days of treatment, Stasov noted, Musorgsky had begun to tell his visitors that "his whole life he had never felt as good as at this moment."[11]

At first, the medical diagnosis was unclear. Stasov, overworked and efficient as always but clearly exhausted by this unexpected new crisis, wrote Balakirev a progress report, not without some frustration. "He looks as if nothing were the matter with him and now recognizes everybody," Stasov reported, "but he talks the devil knows what nonsense and tells impossible stories. They say that besides the epilepsy and strokes he is also a bit mad. He's done for – although he may linger on (so the doctors say) for a year, or maybe only for a day . . . (and can you imagine, yesterday at Leonova's, in the interval between his second and third stroke, he was already asking for wine!!!)."[12]

A sickbed becomes a deathbed only in retrospect. For the next three

23 Repin's portrait of Musorgsky, March, 1881

weeks, it seemed as if Musorgsky would recover; in the sanitary conditions of the hospital, his organism rallied. Only later did conversations carried on with his friends at this time take on a prophetic
finality. One such "prophetic conversation" became especially precious to Golenishchev-Kutuzov, who accorded it much weight in his
memoirs. Sharing with his poet friend his hopes for the future,

Musorgsky confided that he would like to take on "something big," a "fantastic drama," something "totally new that I have never touched before" – because, he confessed, "I would like to take a rest from history, and in general from this all-pervasive prosiness [prozishcha], which won't let you catch your breath" (MR, 98). That indeed was the image of Musorgsky that Kutuzov wished to take away with him. The rest of the world took away Repin's portrait.

Repin heard about Musorgsky's illness from the newspapers. In mid-February he sent Stasov his condolences, adding that "it was such a pity, this brilliant power that was so foolish about taking care of itself physically."[13] One is tempted to believe that Repin, a portraitist of genius, could sense mortality. Sittings for the portrait (there were four in all) began in early March. That week Tsar Alexander II, Liberator of the Serfs, was assassinated. Conversation in the sickroom was totally taken up with the national crisis. As a precaution, Musorgsky's will was drawn up and certified, even though the sick man's health was improving. He could again read books and newspapers; on his bedside table lay Berlioz's *Treatise on Orchestration*. His forty-second birthday was approaching. Filaret came by the hospital and left some money for his brother. At this point, the legends take over.

Some visitors recall the patient clear-eyed and vigorous until the end; others maintain that he was always on the verge of delirium and collapse. One unconfirmed version of the end (widespread in the necrologies and repeated by Repin) was that Musorgsky slipped the money from his brother to an orderly, who brought him a bottle of cognac to celebrate his birthday (for "the heart is not a stone"). Musorgsky drank it down, and paralysis of his arms and legs began to set in. For two days he was fully alert – but in agony. Aleksandra Molas, the elder Purgold sister who, before her marriage, had watched Modest Petrovich so hopefully for signs of his affection, related in her memoirs that according to the nurse's aide on duty when Musorgsky died (late at night, 15–16 March), his final words had been: "It's all over. Oh, how miserable I am!" (MR, 111). The next morning, the

St. Petersburg music critic Mikhail Ivanov stopped by the hospital with birthday greetings. He collided with Golenishchev-Kutuzov in the doorway of the sickroom. "You wish to see Musorgsky?" the Count said in distress. "He's dead."

After Kutuzov moved out to get married in 1875, Musorgsky had written to Stasov: "You have to die alone anyway, not everyone can cross over with me." This crossing-over had now been accomplished. The attention and confusion that followed in the wake of Musorgsky's "passage" was probably inevitable, given the dead end most of his friends had come to see in his life. Even the funeral was somehow an amateur affair, under the drizzling rain: wreaths arrived in large numbers but for some reason there was no singing; the procession was uncertain of the route to the cemetery; during the church service, no one remembered to pass out candles; and even Stasov, almost never at a loss for words, was silent at the grave.

On 20 March, Liudmila Shestakova sent Stasov her packet of letters from "our dear Musinka." She lamented the fact that she had not visited him in time, since he had written that he would be out of the hospital and calling on her in a few days. She then added: "This is an irreplaceable loss for art and for his friends; but for his own future, there was nothing better in view" (L, 415–16). To what extent this sentiment was quietly shared by the other members of his circle is difficult to say. Creative strategies for ensuring Musorgsky a functional life appeared to have reached their end. As if in compensation, there immediately emerged a protective concern for the manner of his death.

Mikhail Ivanov, the music critic who had called too late at the hospital, wrote a frank obituary the following day in which he attributed the cause of death to "that sad propensity which has ruined so many gifted Russians," an addiction to alcohol.[14] Stasov was furious. The drinking was a private matter, he felt, not to be mixed in with the art. In his necrology, he laid fatal blame on "erysipelas of the leg" – and there were other morally acceptable candidates: paralysis of the spine, an adipose heart. According to one eyewitness at the memorial service, Stasov angrily and publicly dressed down Ivanov right there in church for revealing unseemly details about the personal life of the deceased (MR, 145). Repin entered the debate on Ivanov's side. He wrote to Stasov in June that concealment was senseless; it was a fact known to everyone that Musorgsky had become a "half-idiot with shaking hands." But the patriarch was not to be mollified. Indefatigable, possessive, in his own way selfless, Vladimir Stasov was no artist himself – but part of what he understood as his service to art, like leading Musorgsky to Liszt, was to mold (and to the very end) the great artists whom he sponsored. Ivanov never forgave Stasov the offense of that public rebuke. In 1909, three years after the venerable critic died, Ivanov remarked in print that Stasov's "violent attacks against all who refused to believe everything that he shouted about Musorgsky" actually alienated people from the composer, fostered a climate of indifference toward him and his work, and contributed to his early death (MR, 140).

What do we owe an artist like Musorgsky, when we set out to commemorate his life? Can the public legacy of a creator be cleanly separated from private travail, and is it honorable and desirable to do so? This issue is not easily resolved, especially – as shall be seen in the Epilogue – in a culture like the Russian, which has long mythologized its cultural figures. The eminent literary historian Prince D. S. Mirsky called Musorgsky "the greatest Russian tragic poet of his period."[15] And the epithet is sound, if we acknowledge the peculiar "laughter through tears" that made Gogol's sense of the comic so bewitchingly attractive to Musorgsky. Of a biography that offers such personal tragedy and collapse of potential, there are really only two issues that must be confronted at the end: responsibility ("who is to blame?") and survival. How has he continued to live?

The glorious survival of Musorgsky's work, in its multiple versions and magnificent revivals, is not a story that needs retelling here. The issue of responsibility – or less kindly, of blame – is more fraught. Throughout his life, Musorgsky was excruciatingly distressed by death. The loss of his mother, of Viktor Hartmann, of Nadezhda Opochinina, of Osip Petrov was simply unacceptable to him. All accounts agree that alongside their graves Musorgsky sobbed like a child, took to drink, blamed himself for inattentiveness or lack of love, eventually created some piece of music where each could be remembered and revived. These tactics held for a time. But then he came to feel, as he did with Hartmann's death, that yes, the existence of a creation was indeed precious, but that the loss of a *creator* (the process of creativity cut down by death) was nevertheless a tragedy in the face of which there was not, and should not be, any consolation.

Is there responsibility and blame to be fixed anywhere in Musorgsky's own tragically premature death? It seems not. The old scapegoats – the Imperial Theatre Directorate, the tsarist bureaucracy, the need to make a living, a rapacious brother, the Guards regiment that "forced him to drink" – have become thin and unwarranted pretexts. In crucial ways, Musorgsky could not adjust to the economic conditions of post-Emancipation Russia. His personal needs were such that again and again, he ended up alone. He heard combinations of sounds that his fellow musicians did not hear, but he had neither the temperament to explain this inner world to them (in or out of music schools) nor the stamina to sustain his creative vision without their support. The only blame that can be rightly laid at the door of his circle of friends – which, by the end, was his only family – is this: they believed that he had no further potential, that there was nowhere for him to go. And so no one wept at losing him – at losing his person as *creator* – the way Musorgsky would have wept had they been taken, and he been left alive.

Epilogue: the Musorgsky problem, then and now

Under her old regimes both tsarist and Communist, Russia was a saint-building culture. Heroes and martyrs, somewhat like laws in the more impersonal modern state, have helped this immense country to cohere. Russia's vast, vulnerable plain also increased the attractiveness of closed models of history, in which the end (rather than some mythic origin or some malleable, pragmatic middle) bestowed meaning. In such a country, apocalypse often becomes a popular theme; poets and artists easily become prophets. They are called upon to shape national identity "aesthetically," in a visionary and unitary way, when repeatedly an irrational politics, poverty, massive distances, and the constant threat of invasion produce intolerably high levels of insecurity.

Russia's artists became important in other ways as well. Beginning with the sixteenth century, the "exceptionalist" idea enjoyed wide popularity among ideologues of both Church and State. Russia, they believed, was so impenetrable a place and possessed such unusual virtues that she could not be measured by any merely universal standard. Although she carried a message that was destined to save the world (this article of faith was crucial), the outside world, in its fallen state, was not qualified to grasp that message or pass judgment on it. As in many nations on the periphery, the cultured classes of Russia were highly cosmopolitan (they spoke French as a matter of course and often German or English as well, for few Europeans bothered to learn

Russian): did this not make Russia the universal clearing house, the site of the most sophisticated synthesis? Thus, anxieties about backwardness and inferiority merged into a complex of superiority. By the nineteenth century, this presumption of being out of step with Europe, misunderstood, "untranslatable," "colonized" by the more secure, economically advanced cultures to the west while at the same time threatened by savage peoples to the east and south, had become common currency in discussions of "Russianness." Notions of special persecution persisted, even as Russia's most articulate spokesmen never doubted that their country's mission was a chosen one, and as Russia herself continued uninterruptedly to amass the largest land empire the world has ever known. Creative artists were called upon to provide keys to the mystery of their nation's elusive core.

Musorgsky, in part willfully and in part because of posthumous treatment, contributed to this exceptionalist tradition with his music. It has been seen as disobedient, exotic, primitive, saturated with the peculiarities of Russian history and speech. But not only the music has been weighed in the scales of Russia identity. Musorgsky himself became the embodiment of misunderstood, untranslatable genius, the prototypical soul of the Russian land, a martyr for art. Only in the 1980s was this canonical biography (or better, secular hagiography) challenged in any serious way. The chief revisionary architect in the West has been Richard Taruskin. Taruskin's 1993 book on Musorgsky opens with the chapter "Who Speaks for Musorgsky?" – and its thesis, foundational for the present biography, might be summarized here.[1]

Taruskin begins his reading of Musorgsky's life by declaring, in effect, a rebellion against Repin's famous portrait. Painted from life only days before the composer's death, it shows a man in extreme physical decay: propped up, in a hospital robe, seedy, bloated, unkempt, wild-eyed. Projecting back in time from this portrait, it is all too easy to imagine an entire life lived in its desperate spirit. Musorgsky becomes the very image of the idiot savant, hounded by hostile critics and driven to drink, a man who, although in lucid moments able to jot down masterpieces, could never have developed his gifts by disciplined, deliberate choice among musical resources. Yet this canonized image makes a travesty of the composer's fastidious manuscripts, his prodigal technique as a performer, his complex philosophical intelligence, and (until the final years) his almost dandified physical person. For as long as possible in this "Musical life," Repin's portrait was kept out of view.

But why, we must ask, has Repin's visual image haunted us for so long? What image of the composer does it reinforce – and what, in a more just world, might replace it? It is foolish to claim, of course, that the composer was not deficient in certain areas of the European composer's inherited craft (or perhaps simply uninterested in acquiring those skills), or that he did not, at the end, succumb to drink. Taruskin and other revisionists do insist, however, that functional harmony as worked out by the Western tradition is not the only "technique" that submits to discipline or admits of larger design, and that Musorgsky's bad personal habits can be, and were, manipulated by ideologues who wrote their own wish lists into the composer's priorities and creative search. As Taruskin observes, it was Musorgsky's fate to be continually, heroically "rescued" – and rescuers, for all the valuable services they perform, are always mediators (and meddlers). The story of the mediations (or meddlings) of Rimsky-Korsakov in the life of Musorgsky's manuscripts and scores after 1881 is justly famous. But the refashioning of the composer's forty-two lived years is less well known, primarily because it was so wholly successful.

In the realm of biography, as these chapters have shown, the prime "rescuer" was Vladimir Stasov. He responded early to Musorgsky's need for a loyal friend who would provide guidance and extend unconditional trust. When Musorgsky faltered, the older man, his *généralissime*, moved in with praise, hectoring advice, consolation – and often with unwelcome themes and plots. When Musorgsky died, Stasov commemorated his dead friend with several authoritative essays, in which he divided the composer's biography into three phases. The first, 1858–64 (age 19 to 25) was the period of apprenticeship. The second, from 1865 to the mid-1870s (age 26 to 35) was the zenith of

Musorgsky's strength and originality. From then on until the death (phase three, age 35 to 42), a weakening of creative powers and a physical decline set in, dues that are registered in Repin's portrait. One glance at this trajectory reveals that Musorgsky's "peak period" is also the peak of Stasov's influence over him, and, conveniently for the scheme, also the time of Musorgsky's most acclaimed public successes. But Stasov's three-phase model accounts for certain masterpieces (such as *Khovanshchina, Songs and Dances of Death, Without Sun*) so poorly that it must not be taken on faith.

Without denying the mid-life triumphs or the final collapse, Taruskin examines other allegiances in Musorgsky's last decade that might compete with Stasov's rise-and-fall model and loosen its grip. He finds a strong contender in the person of Golenishchev-Kutuzov. Despite the pain Musorgsky suffered when the poet moved out, the two men remained close friends until the composer's death. Kutuzov's personality and aesthetic credo, as we have seen, could not have been further from Stasov's. He was lyrical, aristocratic, a believer in "art for art's sake," and to him the flurry of "intelligentsia aesthetics" that peaked in the 1860s was a barbaric abomination. In his politics, he was imperial (he became an intimate at court and eventually personal secretary to the dowager empress). He was closest to Musorgsky during the latter's so-called years of decline. And he was so astonished, upon reading Stasov's obituaries, that he determined to write a counter-memoir to set right the image of his unfortunate friend. This document, not published during Kutuzov's lifetime, was discovered only in 1935, long after Stasov's views had been co-opted by the Bolsheviks to produce the officially approved, anti-tsarist, proto-revolutionary martyrology of Musorgsky's life for a Soviet readership.

Golenishchev-Kutuzov insisted that Musorgsky was – like himself – an aristocrat in temperament as well as by genealogy. Had he been left on his own, he would have eschewed crude program music and musical buffoonery and developed his natural lyrical gift. But the composer had fallen under the sway of fanatical realists in the 1860s, and he was only just beginning to break free from their tutelage when illness cut him down. The Count thus offered a second trajectory for Musorgsky's life: not a rise-and-fall, but an impeded (although steady) rise. In support of this model, he pointed to the cycles *Songs and Dances of Death* and *Without Sun* (both of which were written to his own verse), as well as to the growing mellifluousness of *Khovanshchina*, an opera that was developing counter to Stasov's advice. Although he sides with the Count, Taruskin reminds us that both Stasov and Golenishchev-Kutuzov were in varying degree unreliable and conjectural as memoirists. Neither friend was disinterested, as indeed no friend can be. And also – no small matter – neither was a practicing musician or composer. The fact that the most powerful shapers of Musorgsky's biography had little or no training in the nuts and bolts of his creative medium should give us pause.

This "competition of biographical images" has enjoyed a peculiar fate in the Soviet and post-Soviet period. In the 1980s, Russians observed a "Musorgsky Decade" in one compact stretch: the centennial of his death in 1981 and the sesquicentennial of his birth in 1989. By a happy accident of history, these two jubilees fell out on either side of the point of no return in the disintegration of the Soviet Empire. Exemplary mythmaking occurred in both halves of the decade, although of wholly different kinds.

The death centenary, planned and prepared during the late Brezhnev years, was celebrated in the elevated, sanctimonious style of Communist jubilees. Major new productions of the operas were mounted. Efforts were renewed to fund and equip the Musorgsky museum (founded in 1978) in Naumovo, Pskov province, not far from the composer's birthplace. The musical press made much of the launching, at last, of an academy edition of Musorgsky's works. But the image of the composer in 1981 was essentially what it had been four decades earlier, during the Stalin-era centennial of 1939. Modest Musorgsky – like Ilya Repin in portraiture or Vasily Vereshchagin in war canvases – was a "realist" artist, a believer in the Russian folk (and concomitantly, in Russia's dark but great destiny), an untutored genius who, having nourished himself with native musical forms, had little need of rigid "Germanic" rules and could loudly dismiss them (as indeed he did) as constricting and corrupting. What is more, Musorgsky's miserable bohemian life under the tsarist regime, while not exactly condoned, was cast as involuntary, perhaps even as inevitable given the injustice of Russian social and professional orders at that time.

Musorgsky (so the canonical biography continued) was the victim of a malign Imperial Theatre Directorate that rejected – or routinely subverted – his radically innovative works. He was ill-served by friends upon whom he depended, devastated at regular intervals by the death or departure of those close to him, and thus he "fell in" to unfortunate habits. As a landowner of modest means impoverished by the emancipation of the serfs, he was forced to take a real job (not a gentleman's sinecure) in various bureaucratic offices and actually turn up at it. The aggrieved tone of these apologies in Soviet scholarship is worth noting. It is characteristic, but something of a surprise to readers outside this tradition, that hardworking Russian servants of culture – including the Soviet "Musorgsky industry" – so intensely protect their poets and musicians from routine institutional obligations, from normal instances of loss, from responsible choice in the face of the facts of life, even as they indulge them in all manner of undisciplined behavior. Although surely preferable to an ethos that deconstructs or taunts past genius with present-day values (which is more of a Western vice), Russian protectiveness toward the personal idiosyncrasies of cultural figures is part of a saint-building impulse. It has infantilized Musorgsky's image.

By 1989, four years into glasnost and already the beginning of the end, a new phase in the consideration of Musorgsky's life and works had begun.[2] As black holes were filled in and criminal deeds in the Soviet past brought to light, the gift of prophecy was sought in two dark geniuses of the nineteenth century – Dostoevsky and Musorgsky. During the initial years of the Gorbachev thaw, there was no essential shift in the prototypical image of the Russian artist as seer, saint, and prophet (that demythologization would begin only later); *what* the artist saw and prophesied, however, was newly configured. In this context, Musorgsky's fate was perhaps a foregone conclusion. Having been cast for so many decades as harbinger of a more hopeful future, as a populist composer, even (on the strength of the insurrectionary final scene in *Boris Godunov*) as a Bolshevik *avant la lettre*, he suddenly became a prophet of Stalinist horrors, a grim Cassandra. It was remarked that Musorgsky's two great historical operas, each set during a *smuta* ["Time of Trouble"], present an honest picture not only of the past but also of the brutal, sterile, ominous future. As Gorbachev's reforms faltered and he himself fell from power, the awful cyclicity of Russian history seemed to reassert itself. Eager to place the unnameable turmoil in a familiar "aestheticized" context, many Russians began to refer to their present as another *smuta*.

In a country already partial to closed models of history and accustomed to burdening art with a real-life subtext, uneasy parallels were not difficult to draw. Take the most famous of Russian operas, *Boris Godunov*. Its plot is paradigmatic – and for many post-Soviets, satisfyingly punitive. A long, heroic, destructive reign of a medieval tyrant (Ivan the Terrible, Stalin) is followed by a period of stagnation. Then, to the relief of the educated classes and to the confusion of the commons, a Westernizing ruler is "elected" according to a new definition of legitimacy (in both 1598 and the early 1990s, a variant of "divine right" is challenged: Boris Godunov becomes Russia's first elected tsar when the ancient dynasty dies out, and Boris Yeltsin is elected to office after forcing the Communist Party to relinquish what it had insisted was its historically mandated monopoly on power). Natural and economic disasters abound. Physical disintegration of the country is followed by a resurgence of national feeling and by a sense that earlier times, however awful, were more tolerable. Back then, Russia was not exposed as hopelessly backward to the rest of the world and the myth of her special status among nations had been sustained.

As Russians strove to understand their present turmoil through their classic works of art, Musorgsky's biography could only accrue also in the spirit of his literary source Pushkin: the common people in those choruses are vigorous, cynical, highly interesting, not easily bullied – but by that token also not easily rallied to a single political cause.) There were productions of Musorgsky's lean, declamatory "original" Boris of 1869, essentially a chamber drama, or perhaps a passion play with music, ending on the death of a conscience-stricken tsar. For the new image of Musorgsky as chronicler of sinners and martyrs, it was perfect.

This elevation of religious motifs and demotion of the radical-populist message was then applied in earnest to the composer's own biography and creative psychology. To be sure, evidence could only be personal, emotional, intuitive. The composer Georgii Sviridov vaguely compared Musorgsky's composing practice to a type of pray-ing, in which an "inner epiphany" was opposed to the "rationalized" symphonic logic common in Western schools.[3] But this mythology too began to pall, and soon a counterwave set in. During a 1989 con-ference near the composer's birthplace in Velikie Luki, several dele-gates asked why, if Musorgsky was a Christian proselytizer, God was so manifestly absent from Boris Godunov, both from Russia's future and from the Holy Fool's lament.[4] By now, revisionism had pulled everything into its corrosive wake. Musorgsky offered no faith in God, in People, in History, just as earlier he had professed no faith in the rudiments of symphonic development. On balance, Musorgsky must be counted among the most contrary nationalists that Russia has produced.

The bias of the present biography was the next step, after a sleuth of Taruskin's caliber had cleared the way and the centennial jubilees had run their course. It suspended judgment on the most contended, least documented aspects of his life: his spiritual beliefs, his politics, and – that perpetual stumbling block – the nature of his personal intima-cies. It strove to avoid endorsing wholly either the Stasov or the Golenishchev-Kutuzov line. In fact, it tried to downplay altogether the model of thinking so familiar in accounts of Musorgsky's life (and encouraged also by the needful tone of his correspondence), namely:

evolution in terms of local influence. Musorgsky was both stubborn and accommodating, which confused his friends. He would listen patiently and then ignore; invite commentary and then fob it off; politely put up with the most carping criticism by uncomprehending mentors and then go his own way. Although he craved and courted the support of others, he never put himself passively under an influence.

For "influence" remains the most problematic of all factors implicated in that definition which Musorgsky made famous: "art is a means of conversing with people." How the composer understood "conversation," how he integrated (and resisted) his immediate musical environment, was often resolved one way in his rhetoric, another in his music. Musorgsky struck out against established Western procedures (the "German School of composition" and its repressive "laws") in a colorful, aggressive manner – in part to clear the field for experiments that might lead to new laws of his own, in part to gratify his like-minded friends, in part simply in keeping with his punchy epistolary style – but such well-advertised rejections cannot undo his profound and formative debts to Western masters, fully traceable in the music. He loved Russian folk culture, had internalized many of its sounds, and wished to show Russia "as she was, in bast sandals" – but he never aimed to transcribe, with ethnographic accuracy, its melismatic songs, modal harmonies, or the archaic melodic formulas of the Church chant. In Musorgsky's case as in all cases of creative genius, any given work of art could be stifled, underrealized, imperfectly expressed. But none of his mature works was the product of passive "influences" or reflexes at either extreme, whether of imitation or rejection. His "conversations" with his surroundings were not dictated by the need to keep loneliness at bay or to keep a foot in the door of the theatre directorate. Personal needs of this sort are impatient, and thus they tack about among ready-made alternatives. To move beyond the ready-made, one must begin not with neediness but with strengths.

The brief "Musical Postlude" following this biography comments on some of the strengths of Musorgsky's tonal imagination, as it chose among the givens of its musical era and assembled its own inventory with which to create. In closing, we might make one final observation about this musical legacy. When the academy edition of Musorgsky's works in thirty-four volumes was announced in 1989 – then postponed to 1992, then delayed for lack of funds until 1996, when volume 1 at last appeared – there was earnest discussion about the proper format for presenting editions, versions, and fragments.[5] The editors were faced with the major, quite unprecedented problem of many works left incomplete, a large number of which were then reworked by other, highly skilled hands. To further "edit" the manuscripts would be unprofessional and disrespectful at this stage in the composer's posthumous career. But to deny a place to Rimsky-Korsakov's versions of the operas, or to Ravel's orchestration of *Pictures from an Exhibition*, would be to exclude musical works of the masterpiece class that *have become* Musorgsky, an integral part of his reception history and legacy. The Academy editors eventually resolved to publish and provide commentary for both the unaltered authorial originals and, in a parallel series, for Musorgsky's compositions "in their creative reworking and orchestration by outstanding musicians." Surely this is the correct solution to what has been a vexed and embittered polemic. For as we have seen, textological – and biographical – writing on Musorgsky has tended to take sides. One is expected to be "for" or "against" the original Musorgsky scores, for or against Rimsky-Korsakov's (or Ravel's) more brilliant-sounding adaptations. Operatic legend is rich in anecdotes about famous singers (Fyodor Chaliapin, for one) who refused to perform if a given production (in the above case, the Diaghilev Paris premiere of *Khovanshchina*) was disloyal to a preferred version. In Musorgsky's life more than others', words like "treason" and "betrayal of the author" are commonplace.

But should not our wonder and surprise go the other way? Listen to *Pictures from an Exhibition* for keyboard, and then for orchestra; experience Rimsky-Korsakov's 1908 version of *Boris* in one mood and the author's 1874 original in another. All of them are tremendously good.

Musical postlude: appraising the artistic product

David Geppert

Apart from appraising an artist's stratagems for personal survival in society, one might also appraise his artistic product by what he chooses from available resources, and by how he processes his choices according to his abilities and ideals – somewhat like a chef who shops in a country market, and then returns to his kitchen to prepare his specialty. His choice of resources will involve embracement, acceptance, indifference, and rejection. His processing will involve his technical strengths and weaknesses, and also the thrust of his ideals – these being perhaps the distillation of many previous choices and processings, but now elevated to a determining role. The artistic product itself is a small world, presumably reflecting in vivid fashion some larger world. As long as the artist believes in his product's potential, he will protect it as a mother hen her chick, and he will curry favor if he feels their survival depends upon such behavior. Apparently Musorgsky was like this. But here we are concerned with an appraisal of his artistic product.

For venturesome European composers living in the first half of the nineteenth century, the secure establishment of a tuning system called equal temperament was a promising resource. It offered a finite but unbounded domain of twelve chromatically equidistant tones for each octave, free of any horridly out-of-tune interval, a domain wherein a pioneer could explore and exploit a multitude of exotic as well as orthodox relationships, existing among the twelve transpositions of the traditional diatonic scale of seven tones. Such relationships would be both melodic and harmonic. For Musorgsky – a wonderfully perceptive listener and fluent pianist – the varieties of interconnectedness must have been fascinating and clear.

Also for Musorgsky, these relationships were cast in an additional dimension – that of the traditional modes, whereby any diatonic scale could generate a feeling of "key" (or "tonic" or "final") for any one of its seven tones – not just for the two tones that were considered keynotes respectively for the conventional "major" and "minor" keys. This modal resource was available to Musorgsky by way of Russian folk song and Russian Orthodox chant, as well as by way of their more sympathetic harmonizations. Such sympathetic treatment would have honored the modal transience and ambiguity of folk song or chant, and this kind of subtlety of key feeling dovetailed well with the subtlety of key feeling generated by modulation from one diatonic scale to another; the subtleties were synergistic within the realm of tone, a realm furnished by equal temperament and aerated through this modal dimension.

The melodies in Musorgsky's solo songs show an amazing range of style: patter songs, dramatic songs, lyric songs. Their emotional range is also broad. Sometimes the European influence seems strong, but usually a native element prevails. And there is such a wealth of imagination and verve. The piano accompaniments are both sensitive and vigorous, in a refreshingly gutsy way. In his operas, the aria-like melodies seem not so different from Italianate melody of the time, except for modal influence and more venturesome modulation. His recitative-like melodies, together with the intermediate arioso type, again do not seem so different from European models, except for the same idiomatic extensions. These latter melodic types benefited from an extreme apprenticeship to which Musorgsky had subjected himself, in pursuit of the optimally effective setting of words to the inflections of pitch and rhythm. In his operas as in those composed by some others, certain melodic motives are associated with certain characters in the drama, and with certain of their actions, emotional states, and mutual conflicts.

Musorgsky obviously availed himself of the harmonic resources offered by the European tradition – essentially tertian harmony with various kinds of triads and seventh chords, occasionally a triad with added sixth, occasionally a seventh chord with added ninth. He seemed aware of all the wrinkles, such as a peculiar kind of four-tone chord containing two tritones a major third apart and thus having all its tones in the same whole tone series: the so-called French augmented sixth chord. Of the traditional non-chord tones, he used mostly passing tones and neighboring tones – as did every composer – and occasionally he used suspensions, a more provocative type of non-chord tone. He used pedal points to stabilize key feeling when chords were moving too fast to suggest it, or when profuse figuration or ornamentation, or heavy percussive effects, clouded the harmonic horizon. More idiosyncratically, he occasionally featured "two-tone chords," consisting solely of the initial interval of a third between chordal root and third degree, but with this intervallic third doubled in octaves for a massive effect, and sometimes with such doubled thirds "planed" (that is, moved in parallel motion up or down), suggestive of a lumbering giant.

In my opinion, Musorgsky used his chords with great aplomb – both individually in their pitch distributions and jointly in their progressions. Within a given scale, the traditional movement of chordal roots known as functional harmony (for example, I–IV–V–I) was not cultivated as exclusively by Musorgsky as by conventional composers. Although Musorgsky could use these conventional progressions with clarity and imagination, he also developed progressions that more liberally involved other, less trite Roman numerals of the scale, thereby suggesting more transience and ambiguity of key feeling, recalling the sympathetic harmonizations of folk song and chant. Moreover, he became adept at maneuvering from one type of triad to another, or from one type of seventh chord to another, by engaging one or more voice-parts in chromatic motion while others held firm – sometimes in conjunction with strong chordal root movement by interval of a third, rather than by the more conventional interval of a fifth. Such harmonic progression, both slippery-smooth and incisive, could produce chromatic nuance within a prevailing key or provide startling modulation to another key. Musorgsky also was impressive in varying the *rate* of chord change – the so-called harmonic rhythm – a tactic that produced great dramatic effect.

Something more should be said about Musorgsky's key feeling or tonality: its frequent transience and ambiguity were most often only at the short-term surface of the tonal texture; a more enduring key feeling or tonality tended to prevail beneath the surface. (This condition is spoken of as if it were acoustically objective, when I should concede that it is essentially subjective.) Be that as it may, according to the scrupulously researched convictions of Robert Oldani, Musorgsky often maintained a strong allegiance to a certain keynote or tonic tone for long stretches of music within an operatic scene – even with one such tonic (and mode) being a kind of "framing" tonic (and mode) for the scene's beginning and end. Oldani claims more, citing the consistent correspondence between a particular major or minor key and a particular character in the drama, or between a particular major or minor key and a particular function of one character vis-à-vis another. All this is very persuasive.

Perhaps we could summarize this matter by saying that tonality in Musorgsky's music tended to be a hierarchical affair, cultivated over a broad spectrum ranging from simplicity to complexity at various times, and no doubt with dramatic intention. But rarely was Musorgsky so confusedly complex as to suggest atonality – although of course approaches to this state also could have their dramatic impact.

With reference to Musorgsky's qualities as a composer, as distinct from those as a dramatist, some musicians have contended that he was indifferent to certain important aspects of the Western musical tradition, and even that he willfully rejected some of them. Musorgsky contended as much himself, in acrimonious remarks, and seemed rather proud of his selectivity. His critics faulted him largely in terms of his musical texture and continuity: he was not careful enough in his fashioning of the auxiliary voice-parts; their linear integrity was not always honored; sometimes they were crude. Again, his musical phrases were too erratic, and they did not combine into larger symmetrical periods. His musical ideas were not logically or thoroughly developed. His orchestration was ineffective.

For an example of such criticism, I quote the concluding sentence in the classic entry on Musorgsky in *Grove's Dictionary of Music and Musicians* (fifth edition, 1954), by Professor Gerald Abraham, founding historian for Russian music in English-speaking lands: "Indeed no musician has been more completely a dramatic composer than Musorgsky; as a musical translator of words and all that can be expressed in words, of psychological states and even physical movements he is unsurpassed; as an absolute musician he is hopelessly limited, with remarkably little ability to construct pure music or even a purely musical texture."

Such criticism seems to me hopelessly uncomprehending in its severity. Against what musical norms was Abraham measuring Musorgsky's music? After all, the nineteenth century was essentially an era of homophonic music. By that time, there already had been great departure from the *a capella* ideal of the sixteenth century, wherein all voice-parts were supposedly of equal significance, and also had to be strictly independent of one another at any moment of the composition – although they imitated one another at various temporal and tonal intervals, subject to strict rules of rhythm and harmony. Similarly, there already had been some departure from the practices of the seventeenth and early eighteenth centuries, wherein a main melodic line was complemented by a vigorously active bass line to produce a contrapuntal envelope, within which there might be just "filler" voice-parts to complete the tertian harmony (often improvised on the keyboard instrument), although usually the envelope enclosed a few contrapuntal voice-parts. Likewise, there already had been some departure from late eighteenth-century symmetries of form, involving phrase, period, and section, as well as from the compulsions of functional harmony that strove to maintain a phrase's key feeling in very obvious ways, and from formulas of key relationship for the total composition – schematics that had become tediously predictable.

By Musorgsky's time, the presence of a prime voice, supported by respectable secondary voices, was generally accepted as adequate musical texture. In more ambitious passages, such secondary voices were countermelodies or even co-equally prime, but often they were just gracefully supportive or decorously imitative, and much of the time they were of minimal contrapuntal interest – in other words, very close to being mere harmonic filler. As such, they were undistinguished rhythmically, but such lack could be compensated for by rhythmic additives of an ornamental or filigree nature, by arpeggiated figures, ostinato figures, or just oom-pah bass figures, busy somewhere in the texture. The very subordinate voice-parts tended to have a short life, bifurcating from and merging with one another, with discreet unconcern. Of course, doubling of voice-parts at the unison or octave was acceptable for purposes of sonority, and heterophony was tolerated, whereby two versions of some voice-part more or less doubled each other – usually the prime voice of the vocal or instrumental solo proceeding in heterophony with some line of the accompaniment.

Such were the standards of practice for the homophonic era. In Musorgsky's musical textures, all such devices occurred. So why was he singled out for criticism? Perhaps his critics thought he blatantly overstepped bounds that already were too lenient, in matters of musical texture and continuity.

First, in some critics' opinions, Musorgsky tolerated awkward linear intervals like augmented seconds and fourths and diminished fourths, in his supportive voices and even occasionally in his prime vocal line. But in Musorgsky's defense, these usually occurred as a consequence of his harmonic choices, coupled with his refusal to circumvent the occurrences by bland linearity or emasculated redistribution of chord tones. Also, the conventional graciousness of voice-leading did not always seem important or even desirable to Musorgsky. He seemed more concerned with the harmonies *as entities of sound* – not necessarily just for their own sake, but more accurately for the sake of programmatic implication, or for the sake of the verbal text, its declamation, and the drama it implied. In other words, the harmonies, either individually or in succession, were directly serving his extra-musical intention by what they were *as sonorous units*, whose significance was in their totality of effect – coming from their intervallic distribution within the pitch registers, their possible ornamentation or figuration, their instrumental scoring together with percussive sounds, their inherent tonal nature arising from their particular recipes of chordal intervals, and their implications for key feeling and modulation. This totality of effect then would enhance the vocal line and intensify its dramatic burden.

Second, in some critics' opinions, Musorgsky's supportive voices did not pay the kind of imitative lip service to the prime voice that conservative composers of his time thought appropriate – a kind of yea-saying deference to the motival attributes of the prime voice that would liken the texture to a well-governed kingdom. But in Musorgsky's defense, this kind of motival kowtowing might have seemed inimical and enfeebling to his dramatic intention, which he thought better served at times by bold and even raw agglomerations of tone.

Third, in some critics' opinions, Musorgsky overindulged the splitting and merging of presumably independent voice-parts, where the consequent loss of identity resulted in parallel unisons and octaves, apparently tolerated in good conscience. Often the entire harmony disappeared in favor of open octave passages, particularly at the end of a phrase, in what must have struck his critics as contrapuntal surrender or harmonic suicide. But in Musorgsky's defense, the maintenance of a consistent texture, in the name of contrapuntal or mock-contrapuntal integrity, or even of harmonic integrity, at times might have seemed to him unnecessary, even prosaic – and such consistency in some cases might have struck him as counter-dramatic.

Fourth, in some critics' opinions, Musorgsky's phrase structures tended to be too asymmetrical, too erratic, choppy, and disjointed, even to lack a proper cadence. But in Musorgsky's defense, chaste phrase contours and balanced phrase combinations might have been much too placid and smug, in their refined elegance and inevitability, to suit his dramatic intention. In the same vein, Musorgsky's wonderful freedom and imagination at phrasal synapses constitute one of the glories of his style; his talent here was profoundly necessary for his success with dramatic continuity – whether or not one confers the label "cadence" upon such sensitive moments. Moreover, by these liberated processes, Musorgsky enormously expanded the horizons of *purely musical* continuity as well.

The last remark suggests that presumably pure music might absorb provocative devices and traits from a music stimulated by, and pledged to serve, overtly extra-musical concerns – those of a programmatic, propositional, or dramatic nature. A musical purist might deplore such possibility of absorption, fearing it as a contamination of a pristine aesthetic realm. But a more lenient musician might hold that the values of such a precious realm already would contain duly abstracted and sublimated influences, previously absorbed from a broader, rougher domain of references. Therefore, it is only personal taste that defines the optimal condition, celebrating aesthetic values refined from a conglomeration of raw references. Musorgsky's taste no doubt inclined toward the worldly referential side, but in my view, he did labor to bring forth an aesthetic transmutation, however much stripped of niceties, frills, and conceits it might have seemed. And his taste preferences have become increasingly welcome to later generations, even surviving the skillful attempts of well-meaning musicians to improve upon his choices.

Perhaps Musorgsky was inclined to accept solutions of musical texture that lay naturally under his hands at the piano, or were derived from distributions that his fingers could cover – in which case the identity of supportive voice-parts could be easily lost, assuming he was considering them at all. Furthermore, a texture bristling with counterpoint might have been too much of a challenge even for a pianist as fabulous as he was, particularly since he also liked to sing the vocal lines in a kind of one-man dramatic projection that apparently satisfied him very much. If such activity seems bizarre, consider that perhaps it was this possibility of projection by himself alone that inspired him to such dramatic heights, enhanced so splendidly by the musical component he concocted. Even as he knew that the eventual product would require the participation of many persons, perhaps for his creative energies "to come to a boil," as he put it, he needed to anticipate this kind of individualized fulfillment.

In the light of such spectacular monologism, I wonder what Musorgsky meant when he said, "Art is a means for conversing with people." It does not seem plausible that he was referring to the conversations or confrontations among his *dramatis personae*, for then his solo songs would not be covered, nor would his instrumental works. And the somewhat non-contrapuntal style of his musical texture would discourage the assumption that he was referring to a kind of *musical* dialogue among the performers themselves. Then again, it would seem trivial if he were referring to pre-performance or post-performance soirées, devoted to discussion of the performance. His remark must have referred to something that should occur during performance itself, between the solo performer or cast of performers and the audience – or by extension, between the authors (composer, librettist, and poet or playwright) and the audience. But traditionally, that situation is one of sole or multiple monologism – the audience is not supposed to talk up or talk back, at least not during performance. What, then, could Musorgsky have meant?

My guess is this: that by the term "conversing," Musorgsky meant a kind of sharing or communing with his audience – albeit in a monologic vein, but nevertheless freed from the oppressive sense of formalist dogma, smug patronization, and downright boredom that he associated with a caricature he dubbed "Germanized music." With the latter, there was no sharing or communing, but rather an *ex cathedra* pronouncing from elite performers to submissive listeners.

Preface

1 A. Gozenpud, *Dostoevskii i muzykal'no-teatral'noe iskusstvo* (Leningrad: Sovetskii kompozitor, 1981), 169.
2 The Yasnaya Polyana visit is described in A. Tumanov, *"Ona i muzyka i slovo . . .": Zhizn' i tvorchestvo A. M. Oleninoi-d'Al'geim* (Moscow: Muzyka, 1995), 115–19.
3 Related by Sergei Bertensson about his father, who was Tolstoy's physician, in "A Personal Note," L, xix.
4 Nikolai Gogol, "Sorochintsy Fair," in *Village Evenings Near Dikanka and Mirgorod*, trans. Christopher English (Oxford University Press, 1994), 33–34.
5 See Leslie Kearney, *Linguistic and Musical Structure in Musorgsky's Vocal Music*, ch. 5, "Music Theory," 186–88. Most musical concepts were taken from German; indigenous works on musical form by Russians in Russia did not appear until the 1890s.

1 *Childhood and youth, 1839–1856*

1 The comment is attributed to the literary critic Valentin Kurbatov, cited in Nikolai Novikov, *U istokov velikoi muzyki* [At the Source of Great Music] (Leningrad: Lenizdat, 1989), 124.
2 See Alexandra Orlova, *Musorgsky's Days and Works: a Biography in Documents* (Ann Arbor, MI: UMI Research Press, 1983; orig. publ. 1963), 626.

3 Orlova, *Musorgsky's Days and Works*, 38.

4 Roald Dobrovenskii, *Rytsar' bednyi: kniga o Musorgskom* [The Poor Knight: a Book About Musorgsky] (Riga: Liesma, 1986).

5 Novikov, *U istokov velikoi muzyki*. Novikov approves of Dobrovensky's "fictionally enhanced biography" on 73–74.

6 For a summary of the story, see Richard Taruskin, "Pronouncing the Name," in *Musorgsky: Eight Essays and an Epilogue* (Princeton University Press, 1993), xxvii–xxxi.

7 Novikov, *U istokov velikoi muzyki*, 23.

8 This information on the Chirikov family life and properties comes largely from Novikov, 115ff.; on Pyotr Alexeyevich, 145ff.

9 My source for the Pskov region musical folklore is G. Golovinskii, *Musorgskii i fol'klor* (Moscow: Muzyka, 1994), 21–23. Quotation on p. 21.

10 See Richard Taruskin, "From Subject to Style: Stravinsky and the Painters," in Jann Pasler, *Confronting Stravinsky: Man, Musician, and Modernist* (Berkeley: University of California Press, 1986), 31. The pioneering Russian ethnographer, Evgeniia Linyova, published her sensational finds between 1897 and 1909.

11 Novikov, *U istokov velikoi muzyki*, 130–54.

12 Dobrovenskii, *Rytsar' bednyi*, 354.

13 For a rehabilitation of the brother, see Novikov, *U istokov velikoi muzyki*, 154–70.

2 *Apprenticeship in St. Petersburg, 1850s–1860s: composers' evenings and the commune*

1 Dobrovenskii, *Rytsar' bednyi*, ch. 5, 167–70.

2 Nikolay Andreevich Rimsky-Korsakov, *My Musical Life* (New York: Vienna House, 1972), 27–34.

3 M. D. Calvocoressi, *Mussorgsky* (London: J. M. Dent and Sons Ltd., 1946), 8.

4 For these details on the effect of the Emancipation on the Musorgsky estates, I draw on Dobrovenskii, *Rytsar' bednyi*, ch. 8, 278–84. Dobrovensky, however, takes the conventional horrified Soviet

stance on Filaret's attitude toward the peasants; my own position is
akin to Novikov's more sympathetic and pragmatic one.

5 For these posts, financial figures, and their embarrassingly low
monetary equivalents, I am grateful to Robert William Oldani's entry
on Musorgsky in the *Revised New Grove Dictionary of Music and Musicians*
(forthcoming).

6 V. V. Stasov, "Modest Petrovich Musorgskii: biograficheskii ocherk"
[first published in *Vestnik Evropy* 5–6 (1881)], in V. V. Stasov, *Izbrannye
stat'i o M. P. Musorgskom* (Moscow: GosMuzIzdat, 1952), 28–242, esp.
p. 51. Excerpts of this lengthy memoir are translated in MR, 8–21 and
in segments and headnotes throughout L (for the passage on the
commune, see L, p. 57).

7 For the revisionist view presented here, I am indebted to arguments
put forth by Andrew M. Drozd in his *Chernyshevsky's "What is To Be
Done?"* (Evanston, Northwestern University Press, forthcoming).

8 Stasov, "Modest Petrovich Musorgskii," 52.

9 Novikov, *U istokov velikoi muzyki*, 84.

10 See Oskar von Riesemann, *Moussorgsky*, trans. Paul England (Knopf
1929/repr. New York: Dover Publications 1971), 48. See also the
succinct n. 64 in Taruskin, *Musorgsky: Eight Essays*, 30–31.

11 "*Delo eto po bab'ei chasti.*" Musorgsky to Balakirev, 19 January 1861, in
L, 35.

12 Stasov, "Modest Petrovich Musorgskii," 22. The Russian "*4-i chasti,*"
"fourth part" (the novel was serialized throughout 1858–59, in four
parts), is mistranslated here and in other editions of the letters as
fourth chapter, which perhaps has contributed to the lack of
attention paid this interesting reference. Considerable attention has
been paid in Goncharov scholarship to the "wife–mother" Agafya
Matveyevna and to Oblomov's own fascination with death and his
quest for the womb, very suggestive for Musorgsky's biography. For
an excellent overview, see John Givens, "Wombs, Tombs, and Mother
Love: a Freudian Reading of Goncharov's *Oblomov*," in Galya Diment,
ed., *Goncharov's "Oblomov": a Critical Companion* (Evanston, IL:
Northwestern University Press, 1998), 90–109.

3 Conservatories, "circles," and Musorgsky at the far musical edge

1 For the full text, see A. G. Rubinstein, "The State of Music in Russia,"
   The Age [Vek], 1 (1861), in Stuart Campbell, ed. and trans., *Russians on
   Russian Music, 1830–1880: an Anthology* (Cambridge University Press,
   1994), 64–73.
2 For Rubinstein's story in the context of the 1850s–70s and on the
   rivalry between Conservatory and Free Russian School, see Robert C.
   Ridenour, *Nationalism, Modernism, and Personal Rivalry in Nineteenth-
   Century Music* (Ann Arbor, MI: UMI Research Press, 1981).
3 Campbell, ed., *Russians on Russian Music*, 67, 69, 73.
4 V. V. Stasov, "Conservatoires in Russia. Comments on Mr.
   Rubinstein's article," *The Northern Bee* [Severnaya pchela], (4, 5, 24
   February 1961), in Campbell, ed., *Russians on Russian Music*, 73–80.
5 Leslie Kearney, "Linguistic and Musical Structure in Musorgsky's
   Vocal Music," Ph.D. dissertation (Yale University, 1992), 29. To
   develop her thesis about process, Kearney draws on the Russian verb
   system (which is more precise about the nature of present-tense
   activity than about differentiated or relative pasts), the weakness of
   Russian abstract nouns, and the effect of stress patterns on the
   Russian worldview (chs. 1–3).
6 V. V. Stasov, "Modest Petrovich Musorgskii: Biograficheskii ocherk,"
   73.
7 Ch. 4: "Who am I? (And Who are You?)", in Richard Taruskin,
   Defining Russia Musically (Princeton University Press, 1997), 70–75.
8 Kompaneiskii sang the song for Serov and recorded his reaction; see
   Kompaneiskii, "Recollections of Musorgsky," in MR, 5.
9 For the rise and fall of Italian opera and a full discussion of its
   reflections in Russian criticism (pro and contra the nationalists), see
   Richard Taruskin, ch. 10, "Ital'yanshchina,'" in Taruskin, *Defining
   Russia Musically*, 186–235.
10 *Marriage*, Act 1, scene 1. Cited here in the translation of Christopher
    English from Nikolai Gogol, *Plays and St. Petersburg Tales* (Oxford
    Classics, 1995), 183.
11 The best discussion of this work and its larger connection to
    Musorgsky's aesthetics is Richard Taruskin, "Handel, Shakespeare,

and Musorgsky: The Sources and Limits of Russian Musical
Realism," in Taruskin, *Musorgsky: Eight Essays*, 71–95.

4 *1868–1874: Musorgsky and Russian history*

1 The most thorough historian of the operatic *Boris* is Robert William
Oldani. See his ch. 4, "History of the Composition, Rejection,
Revision, and Acceptance of *Boris Godunov*" and ch. 5, "A Tale of Two
Productions," in Caryl Emerson and Robert William Oldani, *Modest
Musorgsky & Boris Godunov: Myths, Realities, Reconsiderations*
(Cambridge University Press, 1994). The volume also contains a
survey of censorship documents and selected criticism. For more
detail on the former, see Oldani, "*Boris Godunov* and the Censor,"
19th-century Music, 2 (March 1979), 245–53.

2 For a capsule history of the theatre situation in the capital, see ch. 10
of Taruskin, *Defining Russia Musically*, 186–88.

3 For a detailed motivation of the move from 1869 to 1874 versions, see
Taruskin, "Musorgsky versus Musorgsky," in Taruskin, *Musorgsky:
Eight Essays*, 201–90.

4 Rimsky-Korsakov, *My Musical Life*, 122–23.

5 For an account of this influence, see Taruskin, "The Present in the
Past: Russian Opera and Russian Historiography, circa 1870," parts
VI–VII, in Taruskin, *Musorgsky: Eight Essays*, 176–200.

6 See Oldani, "History of the Composition, Rejection, Revision, and
Acceptance of *Boris Godunov*," in Emerson and Oldani, *Modest
Musorgsky & Boris Godunov*, 89. For the details on financial
remuneration that follow in the text, see 94, 105.

7 G. A. Laroche, "Mr Kondratyev's Benefit Performance at the
Mariinsky Theatre" (excerpts from M. Musorgsky's opera *Boris
Godunov*), in *Golos*, 45 (1873), cited in Campbell, ed., *Russians on
Russian Music*, 225. For Laroche's review of the 1874 premiere, see
ibid., 238–40.

8 For a discussion of Cui's review in *St.-Peterburgskie vedomosti* (6
February 1874) and Musorgsky's letter to Stasov in response to it, see
Emerson and Oldani, *Modest Musorgsky & Boris Godunov*, 102–04; see
also L, 265–67.

9 James H. Billington, *The Icon and the Axe* (New York: Vintage Books, 1970), 395. His Part Five bears a Musorgskian title ("On to New Shores"), and his discussion of populism (esp. pp. 387–416) is the basis for my summary comments. Musorgsky's operas are given an eloquent and strong – if conventional – reading as populist art.

10 The letter, allegedly sent from Adelheid von Schorn to Vasily Bessel on 19 May 1873, was published for the first time in 1932, in Russian "translation" and with a false reference (it appears in L, 207–11). For its exposure as a forgery, see Emil Haraszti, "Trois faux documents sur Fr. Liszt," *Revue de Musicologie*, 42 (December 1958), 202–15, and Marta Papp, "Liszt and Musorgsky: The genuine and the false documents of the relationship between the two composers," *Studia musicologica*, v. 29 (1987), 267–84. I thank Robert Oldani for alerting me to this material.

11 Rimsky-Korsakov, *My Musical Life*, 144.

12 Dobrovenskii, *Rytsar' bednyi*, 544.

13 Rimsky-Korsakov, *My Musical Life*, 144.

14 V. V. Stasov, "Modest Petrovich Musorgskii: Biograficheskii ocherk," 122–23.

15 Musorgsky writes Poliksena Stasova in Vienna, 23 July 1873: ". . . (But Peter and Sofia are kept off stage – this is decided; better without them); and I am eager to do a people's drama – *I am so eager*." In L, 224.

16 Musorgsky to Golenishchev-Kutuzov, 31 July 1877 (L, 360). The comparison here is between *Marriage* and Musorgsky's new setting of Gogol "for the grand stage," *Sorochinsky Fair*.

5 *The 1870s: Musorgsky and death*

1 See Michael Russ, *Musorgsky: "Pictures at an Exhibition"* (Cambridge University Press, 1992), 1–20. Russ is completely correct in arguing that Hartmann was not a politically committed populist or activist. Where Russ errs, in my opinion, is in his conventional assumption that Musorgsky is one. The friendship between the two men – both "cultural nationalists" with aristocratic habits – is easier to explain than Russ makes out.

2 Mikhail Saltykov-Shchedrin, "On the Side: Notes, Sketches, Stories, etc.," in *Otechestvennye zapiski*, 11 (November 1874), in L, 285–86.

3 "Eks" [Alexander Chebyshev-Dmitriev] in *Birzhevye vedomosti*, 336 (10
   December 1872), in Orlova, *Musorgsky's Days and Works*, 284–85.

4 For Borodin's account of this "famous concocted caricature" by the
   Makovskys, a husband-and-wife artist team, see his letter to his wife
   of 4 October 1871, in L, 172–73. See also Shestakova's description in
   "My Evenings," MR, 50–51.

5 For this story, see Elizabeth Kridl Valkenier, *Ilya Repin and the World of
   Russian Art* (New York: Columbia University Press, 1990), "The Break
   with Stasov and the New Aesthetics," 136–38.

6 The so-called *Peredvizhniki* (Itinerants, Wanderers) were a group of
   visual artists allied in spirit with the radical *kuchkist* musicians who
   resisted the Conservatory. In 1863, just before Repin's arrival in St.
   Petersburg, fourteen graduating students of the Imperial Academy of
   Arts, wishing to pursue populist native themes, walked out in protest
   against being assigned a topic from classical mythology for the final
   Gold Medal competition. In 1871 they formed "The Association of
   Traveling Art Exhibits" (hence "Itinerants"), which Repin joined in
   1878.

7 See Vahan D. Barooshian, *V. V. Vereshchagin: Artist at War* (Gainesville:
   University Press of Florida, 1993), 44–47. Also A. K. Lebedev and
   A. V. Solodovnikov, *V. V. Vereshchagin* (Moscow, Iskusstvo, 1988),
   52–58.

8 M. P. Musorgskii, *Pis'ma* (Moscow: Muzyka, 1984), 338.

9 Russ, *Musorgsky: "Pictures at an Exhibition,"* 22.

10 Borodin to Yekaterina Borodina, 25 September 1874, in L, 282.
   Unlike *Songs and Dances*, the cycle *Without Sun* was published in
   Musorgsky's lifetime (Bessel, 1874), but went almost unnoticed.

11 Valkenier, *Ilya Repin and the World of Russian Art*, 39.

12 For Dobrovensky's attempt to negotiate these delicate matters, see
   Rytsar' bednyi, 589–92.

13 Liudmila Shestakova to Vladimir Nikolsky, 23 June 1875, in Orlova,
   Musorgsky's Days and Works, 459.

14 Quoted in L, 301. Dobrovensky questions the timing and authenticity
   of this reminiscence on pp. 590–92.

15 Musorgsky tells the same story to Poliksena Stasova, 26 July 1873,
   and to Stasov, 2 August 1875. In L, 229–32. Quotes in text are from
   the letter to Stasov, 231.

6 *Beyond tragedy: the final years*

1 Vasily Bertenson, from "Sheaf of Recollections," in MR, 121–22; also in L, 351–52.

2 Not surprisingly, it is Golenishchev-Kutuzov in his memoirs who reports Musorgsky's gratitude to Eduard Napravnik, conductor of the Maryinskii Theatre, and the composer's approval of the Kromy cut (MR, 88–89); for Stasov's letter to *Novoe vremia* (27 October 1876), see L, 348–49.

3 See Ivanov's 1909 addendum to his necrologue on Musorgsky in MR, 139.

4 Venedikt Erofeev, *Moskva-Petushki* (1968), quoted here from the translation by H. W. Tjalsma as *Moscow to the End of the Line* (New York: Taplinger Publishing Company, 1980), 79–80.

5 Golenishchev-Kutuzov, "Reminiscences of Musorgsky," in MR, 81–99, esp. p. 98. This hypothesis is corroborated by Richard Taruskin, who argues that Musorgsky was drawn to *Sorochintsy Fair* as part of a move away from individualistic declamation and toward romantic nationalism and folk song – which liberated him from depicting individuals and permitted him the stylized, stereotypical portraiture of ethnic groups. See "Sorochintsy Fair Revisited" in Taruskin, *Musorgsky: Eight Essays*, 328–94.

6 Unsigned review in *Voskresnyi listok muzyki i ob"iavlenii*, 9 (21 January 1879), in Orlova, *Musorgsky's Days and Works*, 557–58.

7 Nikolai Soloviev in *St.-Peterburgskie vedomosti*, 20 (20 January 1879), in Orlova, *Musorgsky's Days and Works*, 557.

8 Nikolai Kompaneiskii gives a moving account of Musorgsky's reaction to "grandpa" Petrov's death in his "Recollections of Musorgsky," MR, 7.

9 Rimsky-Korsakov, *My Musical Life*, 225–26. I have shifted the order of Rimsky's sentences somewhat in this passage.

10 Nadezhda Rimskaya-Korsakova to Vasily Yastrebtsev as recorded in October 1893; in Orlova, *Musorgsky's Days and Works*, 595.

11 V. V. Stasov, "Nekrolog M. P. Musorgskogo" [1881], in V. V. Stasov, *Izbrannye stat'i o M. P. Musorgskom*, 23.

12 Stasov to Balakirev, 13 February 1881, in Orlova, *Musorgsky's Days and Works*, 636.

13 Repin to Stasov, 16 February 1881, in Orlova, *Musorgsky's Days and Works*, 638.
14 Mikhail Ivanov, *Novoe vremia*, 1814 (17 March 1881), in *ibid.*, 647.
15 D. S. Mirsky, *A History of Russian Literature* [1926], ed. Francis J. Whitfield (New York: Vintage, 1956), 255.

Epilogue: *the Musorgsky problem, then and now*

1 Richard Taruskin, "Who Speaks for Musorgsky?", in Taruskin, *Musorgsky: Eight Essays*, 3–37.
2 For this watershed period and the various productions of Boris Godunov that illustrate it, see Taruskin, *Musorgsky: Eight Essays*, 395–407 ("Epilogue: Musorgsky in the Age of *Glasnost*'"); and Emerson and Oldani, *Modest Musorgsky & Boris Godunov*, 278–88 (ch. 10, "Boris Godunov during the Jubilee Decade: the 1980s and Beyond").
3 Georgii Sviridov, "O Musorgskom," in *Nasledie M. P. Musorgskogo: sbornik materialov* (Moscow: Muzyka, 1989), 9.
4 See D. Logbas, "God Musorgskogo prodolzhaetsia: v kontekste XX veka," in *Sovetskaia muzyka*, 11 (1989), 89–91.
5 See V. I. Antipov, et al., "Polnoe akademicheskoe," in *Sovetskaia muzyka*, 3 (1989), 65–77.
6 Milan Kundera, *Testaments Betrayed*, trans. from the French by Linda Asher (New York: Harper Collins, 1993/1995), 273–74; 249. I thank Richard Taruskin for alerting me to this text.

An accurate, fully satisfactory single-volume history of Russian music that would put Musorgsky into context is yet to be written. One serviceable introduction, now outdated, is Richard Anthony Leonard, *A History of Russian Music* (New York: Macmillan, 1968; orig. published 1956). A recent magisterial study that only intermittently addresses Musorgsky but provides the best possible guide to the nation and musical culture that nourished him, is Richard Taruskin, *Defining Russia Musically* (Princeton University Press, 1997).

The following English-language texts are recommended for further inquiry into Musorgsky's life, work, and times:

Brown, Malcolm Hamrick, ed. *Musorgsky In Memoriam: 1881–1981*. Ann Arbor, MI: UMI Research Press, 1982.

Calvocoressi, M. D. *Mussorgsky*. London: J. M. Dent and Sons Ltd, 1946.

Campbell, Stuart, ed. and trans. *Russians on Russian Music, 1830–1880: an Anthology*. Cambridge University Press, 1994.

Emerson, Caryl and Robert William Oldani. *Modest Musorgsky & Boris Godunov: Myths, Realities, Reconsiderations*. Cambridge University Press, 1994.

Kearney, Leslie. *Modest Musorgsky: Poetry, Opera and Song*. Cambridge University Press, forthcoming.

Leyda, Jay and Sergei Bertensson, ed. and trans. *The Musorgsky Reader: a Life of Modeste Petrovich Musorgsky in Letters and Documents*. New York: Da Capo Press, 1970 [orig. published 1947].

Orlova, Alexandra. *Musorgsky's Days and Works: a Biography in Documents*.

Trans. and ed. Roy J. Guenther. Ann Arbor, MI: UMI Research Press, 1983.

Orlova, Alexandra, comp. and ed. *Musorgsky Remembered*. Trans. Véronique Zaytzeff and Frederick Morrison. Bloomington: Indiana University Press, 1991.

Ridenour, Robert C. *Nationalism, Modernism, and Personal Rivalry in Nineteenth-Century Russian Music*. Ann Arbor, MI: UMI Research Press, 1981.

Riesemann, Oskar von. *Moussorgsky*. Trans. Paul England. New York: Dover Publications, 1971.

Taruskin, Richard. *Musorgsky: Eight Essays and an Epilogue*. Princeton University Press, 1993.

Note: Musical and literary works are entered under the appropriate composer or writer; letters (when significant) are noted under their authors. Page numbers for illustrations are given in boldface.